LOVE THIS!

ANDY BRANER

LEARNING TO MAKE IT A WAY OF LIFE, NOT JUST A WORD

LOVE THIS!

ANDY BRANER //////

LEARNING TO MAKE IT A WAY OF LIFE, NOT JUST A WORD

www.invertbooks.com

ZONDERVAN®

ZONDERVAN.com/
AUTHORTRACKER
follow your favorite authors

LOVE THIS! *Learning to Make it a Way of Life, Not Just a Word*
Copyright ©2006 by Andy Braner

Youth Specialties products, 300 South Pierce Street, El Cajon, CA 92020 are published by
Zondervan, 5300 Patterson Avenue Southeast, Grand Rapids, MI 49530.

**Published in association with the literary agency of Alive Communications, Inc., 7680 God-
dard Street, Suite 200, Colorado Springs, Colorado, 80920, www.alivecommunications.com.**

Library of Congress Cataloging-in-Publication Data

Braner, Andy.
  Love this! : learning to make it a way of life, not just a word /
Andy Braner.
    p. cm.
  ISBN-10: 0-310-27380-3 (pbk.)
  ISBN-13: 978-0-310-27380-6 (pbk.)
  1. Love—Religious aspects—Christianity—Juvenile literature.
  I. Title.
  BV4639.B725 2006
  241'.4—dc22

                                                                        2006029318

Web site addresses listed in this book were current at the time of publication. Please contact Youth Specialties via e-mail (YS@YouthSpecialties.com) to report URLs that are no
longer operational and replacement URLs if available.

*Creative Team: Randy Southern, Kristi Robison, Heather Haggerty, Janie Wilkerson, and
SharpSeven Design*
Cover design by SharpSeven Design

Printed in the United States

07 08 09 10 11 12 • 19 18 17 16 15 14 13 12 11 10 9 8 7 6 5 4 3 2 1

TABLE OF CONTENTS

7   CHAPTER 1: THE WORLD'S MOTIVE

27   CHAPTER 2: GOD'S MOTIVE—LOVE

45   CHAPTER 3: LOVING THE HOMELESS

61   CHAPTER 4: LOVING THE HOMOSEXUAL

79   CHAPTER 5: LOVING THE ADDICTED

95   CHAPTER 6: LOVING THE SICK

109   CHAPTER 7: LOVING THE ELDERLY

123   CHAPTER 8: LOVING OTHER RACES

135   CHAPTER 9: LOVING PEOPLE FROM
                     FOREIGN COUNTRIES

149   CHAPTER 10: LOVING YOUR ENEMIES

163   CHAPTER 11: LOVING OTHER CHRISTIANS

175   CHAPTER 12: LOVING THOSE WHO MESS UP

191   CHAPTER 13: NOW WHAT?

/// CHAPTER 1 ///

THE WORLD'S MOTIVE

"Speak up and judge fairly; defend the rights of the poor and needy." (Proverbs 31:9)

Love. It's such an elusive word. I love hip-hop. I love my wife. I love my dog. I love pizza. How can one word be used in so many different ways?

That question is especially important for Christians, who are told that "God is love" and who are instructed to "love others." How are we supposed to interpret love if we can love our neighbor like we love our car? The answer may lie in one of the most famous parables Jesus ever told. Jesus gave us an example of love for the ages. He left no doubt that genuine love—the kind he calls his followers to—is proactive, sacrificial, and risky.

Consider the Jewish man who was traveling through a dangerous region called Samaria.

THE MAN IN THE DITCH

He was on his way home from a relaxing weekend at his family's farmhouse in a small village outside of Jerusalem. The road he traveled was long and dusty. Knowing he had a difficult journey ahead of him, he had set out early in the afternoon.

It was springtime; the weather was nice and cool. As he walked, he sang songs he had learned at the synagogue. He smiled as he recalled how his mother had kissed him goodbye and his father has shaken his hand and said, "I'm proud of you, Son." He thought about the girl waiting for him back in the city. He wondered what the future held for them.

When he reached the halfway point of his journey, he paused at the top of a large hill to admire the beautiful valley below. It was just before dusk, and his feet were tired. Just as he made up his mind to sit down for a rest, he saw someone approaching from the opposite direction. He recalled his father's warnings about criminals who preyed on solo travelers. So the young man kept walking.

The closer he got to the approaching man, the more nervous the young traveler became. He could see that the man had a deep scar running down the left side of his face. The man flashed a cruel grin. His mouth was gapped with empty spaces where his teeth had been.

As they passed, the young man smiled a cordial hello and nodded to ease the tension. He noticed a second man, much younger than the first, approaching

LOVE THIS!

from the same direction. The young traveler's unease grew when the scar-faced man turned around and began following him.

With a mountain on his right and cliffs on his left the young man had nowhere to run. His unease turned into paralyzing fear.

"Hey!" the first man called.

"Where you going, boy?" the second man said in an eerie, sarcastic tone.

The older man suddenly grabbed the young traveler from behind. The second man punched him in the gut. The young traveler dropped to his knees, gasping for breath. The first man kicked him in the head, sending him sprawling to the ground. And for what seemed like hours, the two attackers took turns beating the young man. They kicked him. They punched him. They spit on him. They called him names.

"You filthy JEW! Who gave you permission to walk on this road? Don't you know where you are?" the scarred man screamed uncontrollably in a fit of rage.

Lying on the ground, the young man grabbed his ankles and tried to endure the beating as long as he could. Soon, however, he lost consciousness.

"Get up! Get up!" the attackers snarled. But the young man didn't move. His battered body was streaked with blood from head to toe. His ribs were broken. His face was disfigured. His skin had turned an ugly purplish-blue from the intense beating.

"Get his money," the first man ordered. They took his coin purse and spit on his face. Then they dragged his broken body to a ditch on the side of the road and walked away, counting their money.

"He was weaker than the others," the first man mocked.

"His dad must not've taught him how to fight," the second man added.

"What kind of guy would walk down this road when the whole town knows we're out here?" the first one wondered.

"He must've wanted to see if the stories were real," the second one said. "It's his own fault. Come on, let's eat." The two assailants calmly made their way to town.

Drifting in and out of consciousness, the young man lay in the ditch, waiting for death to take him. Pain throbbed throughout his body. "This is the end," he thought. He prayed for God to take his life—anything to make the pain stop.

Then he heard someone whistling a familiar tune in the distance.

The young traveler managed to open his swollen right eye and saw a man dressed in traditional religious clothing walking toward him. With a sigh of relief, the young man closed his eye and wondered if God had heard his cry. Was this the savior sent from the holy, loving, compassionate God?

The would-be savior, a priest, saw the man lying in the ditch. The priest slowed his pace and cautiously approached the man. Then a thought occurred to him: "I wonder if this is a trap." He remembered that a local carpenter had been robbed in the area. The priest hurried past the spot where the young man lay. He kept his head down, starring at the rocks in the road, in an effort to avoid eye contact with his potential attacker. "Just keep walking," the priest muttered. "Just keep walking."

The young man in the ditch tried to cry out, but when he opened his mouth to scream "Help!" only a faint squeal emerged. The priest looked back for a moment. "Should I?" he wondered. But his fear got the better of him, and he quickly walked away. "I've got to get back to the synagogue," he told himself with the conviction of a good priest.

The man in the ditch helplessly watched the priest disappear over the hill. The pain in his body was getting sharper, and his bleeding wouldn't stop. He thought every heave of his chest would be his last. He prayed again, "God, if you are real, please send someone to help me. I promise to—" Needless to say, the young man made several deals with God that day.

After his prayer he heard someone else approaching in the distance. "Thank you, Lord!" he prayed excit-

edly. "Thank you for your mercy! Thank you for sending help to your lowly, humble servant. I will forever praise you." He tried again to cry out, but only the same high-pitched squeal left his mouth.

As the next would-be savior got closer, the injured traveler could hear him praying. "Oh good," he thought, "it's a religious man—a Levite. I'm saved."

When the Levite saw the young man in the ditch, he stopped cold in his tracks. He adjusted his yarmulke and pulled on the curly ringlets that framed his smooth face. "God of Abraham, help me now," he prayed. "It's obvious that robbers on this dusty road have set a trap for me. You are God above all gods, and you are the great protector. Help me now!"

The Levite pulled out a stick he carried for just such occasions. He knew robbers had no qualms about stealing things from a Levite, and he was determined not to become another statistic. He wasn't going to let some two-bit scam artists ruin his life. And he wasn't going down without a fight. He held the stick with both hands, close to his body, ready for a sudden attack.

The Levite crossed the road in the same place the priest had crossed only moments before. But the Levite's pace was noticeably slower, almost as though he welcomed a fight. He whispered to the man in the ditch, "Come on, if you dare. I'll show you what Levites are made of." He stole a glance at the body in the ditch. The man's disguise was good, the Levite concluded. He really looked like an injured traveler.

The young man in the ditch struggled to breathe. Blood caked his skin. His pain grew more intense by the minute. He tried to throw up but couldn't move his head to the side. He lost control of his bodily functions. He also lost all hope for help. He resigned himself to the fact that he would die in a ditch, covered in his own waste.

But then a third traveler approached. This man was native to the area, so he knew the potential hazards hiding behind each rock. He was a good man. He had a loving wife and three children waiting anxiously for him to come home for dinner. As he walked the dusty road, his thoughts took him to his warm house, filled with laughter.

He didn't notice the figure on the side of the road because it was late and the sun had already faded below the horizon. Lost in his thoughts, he could almost smell the hot bread his wife was baking at home.

The smell was abruptly interrupted by a different odor—one he'd smelled only weeks before. The smell took him back to a field where a small band of Samaritans had risen up in protest of a Roman tax. In a flurry of violence the Romans crushed the uprising until all that remained was an odor: the stench of blood. The unmistakable and inescapable smell of death.

The same odor he'd smelled then assaulted his senses again. He looked around for its source and noticed a dark figure curled up in the ditch. He bent down and saw a man with curly hair matted to his face. The man's eyes were swollen shut, his head was covered with blood, and his leg was bent in a way legs weren't meant to bend. He saw the man struggling to breathe and quickly jumped in the ditch to help.

The smell was awful, but the family man didn't seem to mind. His only desire was to help a fellow human being. Realizing he was the only person on the road at that time of evening, he made an executive decision. He hoisted the injured man on his shoulder and started the long walk home.

Traveling was difficult. Though the young man was thin, the sheer dead weight of an unconscious person proved harder to manage than the man first thought. He was forced to make several stops along the way.

By the time he finally reached the front door of his home, he was several hours late for the evening meal. But when his wife opened the door, instead of scolding him for his tardiness, she realized the immediate urgency of the situation.

Together they carefully carried the young man to their bedroom and laid him down. They wiped the blood from his face. They cleaned him from head to toe. They stitched the cuts on his head. They applied a special home remedy for his swollen eyes. They called the local doctor to set his broken leg and administer medication. They kneeled at the side of the bed and prayed that God would heal the young man. And then they waited.

Days turned into weeks. Weeks turned into months. The couple dutifully continued to change the man's dressings, clothes, and linens. Nursing their visitor back to health became the family's number one priority—because it was the right thing to do. They didn't anticipate any reward. They didn't need to be praised for their heroism. They had found someone who needed help lying in a ditch and knew it was their responsibility to assist him.

One day after three months of providing intensive care, the couple went to the room to begin their daily caretaking duty. There they found the young man sitting up in bed. The couple immediately fell to their knees and thanked God for healing their guest. "To God be the glory for great things he has done," they said.

The young man stared at his hosts in amazement. The man wasn't wearing a traditional yarmulke. The woman wasn't dressed in traditional Jewish clothing. In fact, they didn't look Jewish at all. A silent horror overcame his soul. The man and woman were SAMARITANS!

Samaritan was a code word in New Testament times for "half-breed." Samaritans were a combination of the Assyrian and Jewish races. As such, they occupied the lowest rung of the Middle Eastern social ladder. They were less favored than even women or dogs.

The young man couldn't believe he, a respected Jew, had been rescued by a Samaritan couple. He'd grown up hating Samaritans. His family had taught him to ostracize Samaritan people for their impure genealogical heritage. It was a strict rule of life: Jews never mingled with Samaritans—EVER! Then the young man came to his senses.

If the Samaritans hadn't rescued him from the ditch, he would have died on the side of the road. His mind told him to hate his hosts, but his heart tugged at him to love them. As love slowly began to win the battle inside him, he began to care about his hosts in spite of who they were, in spite of where they came from, and in spite of who they represented. He was grateful for their deeds and longed to know more about them.

"Thank you," he said softly.

Obviously, this is an embellishment of Jesus' parable of the Good Samaritan. You can read the actual text in Luke 10:29-37. Jesus told this story for a reason, and I think we need to understand it from all vantage points.

Though the details of the story are rooted in first-century life in the Middle East, the principle transcends time periods. We Christians need to ask ourselves, "Who are the 'young travelers' of today? Who are the 'priests'? Who are the 'Levites'? And most important, who are the 'Samaritans'?"

THE MODERN-DAY YOUNG TRAVELER

Everyone travels this long dusty road called life, none of us knowing when evil or misfortune will jump out from behind a rock to batter us into a ditch. Depending on the circumstances, the ditch may be a physical problem,

a financial crisis, an emotional breakdown, a spiritual funk, or whatever epic battle life may orchestrate.

After having talked with hundreds of teenagers from all over the world, I can attest to you today that the ditch is a real place where people lie, longing for someone to notice and help them. In the teenage years the ditch may take the form of depression, an identity crisis, or a traumatic relationship with a mother or a father. In the adult years it may take the form of homelessness, prostitution, addiction, or homosexuality. Whatever the case, such issues can keep unsuspecting travelers down for a long time.

Obviously, a lot of people are lying in ditches, waiting for someone to help. The question is, which passerby will you be when you see someone in a ditch?

THE MODERN-DAY PRIEST

"Homeless men are just lazy bums waiting to take your money." "AIDS victims might cough on you—then what?" "Are you ready to live the rest of your life with AIDS? Prostitutes just want to seduce you; stay away!"

Like the priest who passed by the injured traveler, many people walk down life's road with an oppressive fear of every situation and encounter. They disdain anything and everything that resides beyond their comfort zones. If they encounter someone who looks different, smells different, or talks different, their first instinct is to make their way quickly to the other side of the "road," lest they be caught in a compromising position.

It's human nature to judge other people. No matter how hard you try to be impartial, the fact is, you have a set of assumptions that directly influence the way you respond to certain people. If you're honest, you'll find yourself judging other people all the time. And although sometimes it's smart to be aware of things going on around you, taken to its extreme, this thought process merely advocates negligent walking. We leave people stranded in the ditch, longing for someone to jump down there with them and pull them to safety.

Society has trained us to look out for "number one" at all times, and sometimes we justify that attitude by assigning blame. We tell ourselves that people have only themselves to blame for their situations. And we keep on walking. We walk past the homeless guy from fear of what we've heard about the homeless. We walk past sick folks because, after all, we're not doctors—what can we do? We walk past the elderly because they've had a good life, and this is our time!

Society tells us to put on our "priest" clothes and mind our own business—even if people suffer and die as a result. You'd think that Christians would be able to see the danger of such thinking. Unfortunately, that's not usually the case.

You see, Christians are often trained to look alike, talk alike, and act alike. If anyone challenges that sameness—that stereotypical notion of holiness—we

LOVE THIS!

walk past him. We don't want to compromise our own morality by being seen in a ditch, so we don't stop.

A friend of mine works for a teenage ministry in an average-sized city in the Midwest. The ministry is run by a board of directors. Its primary focus is to train and equip teens to understand who God is, how to live a Christian life, and how to share the gospel with their friends.

One Monday night a board member drove to the clubhouse where the teens met and saw a couple of kids out front smoking cigarettes. Fuming with anger, she called the other board members for an emergency meeting. "We cannot allow those kids to be out in front of our ministry," she said. "We don't want our kids to be around 'those' kinds of people."

Talk about traveling with blinders on!

"Those kinds of people" are the ones lying in the ditches of life, looking for something more. They think they've found it in the nicotine buzz; but in reality, they are longing for the satisfaction only the Son of God can give. And often all they need is a friend to say, "Smoking is stupid," to be ready to quit.

The Christian life isn't about stopping only for people dressed in three-piece suits, singing "How Great Thou Art" and chanting "Glory to God." The Christian life is about climbing down into ditches in order to pull people out. Sometimes it's messy work. But contrary to what society would have you believe, helping others isn't a waste of time. In fact, it's one of the biggest sources of satisfaction life has to offer.

THE MODERN-DAY LEVITE

Some Christians walk the road of life holding the proverbial sticks in their hands, ready for a fight. When they hear a word such as *homosexual*, they prepare themselves for spiritual battle.

The Bible makes it clear that Christians are responsible for defending their faith. First Peter 3:15 says, "But in your hearts set apart Christ as Lord. Always be prepared to give an answer to everyone who asks you to give the reason for the hope that you have."

But it doesn't stop there. Look at the last seven words of the verse: "But do this with gentleness and respect." That's the part we sometimes forget. We forget because the world says we have to win arguments at any cost. We forget because we refuse to take any "lip" from anyone. We forget because, after all, "right is right and wrong is wrong."

Words such as *homeless, addict,* and *homosexual* conjure a need in some Christians to protect our spiritual heritage (as though we had anything to do with building our spiritual heritage). We carry a big "stick" of knowledge to beat down anyone who tries to challenge our belief in God or minimize his Word. We need to realize, though, that some people don't know any better. They're lying in a ditch, pleading for us to put down our sticks for a minute and get our hands dirty.

They cry out for help. But many of us walk past without stopping, convinced that they're simply crying wolf.

Like the busy Levite in the parable, we have places to go and people to see. We have no time for certain types of people. We're too busy following the world's M.O. of "looking out for number one"—that is, doing what's best for us.

GOD'S M.O.

I don't blame Christians for being reluctant to help. Looking into the eyes of a drug addict is uncomfortable. It's natural to question your response as a Christian. It's normal to feel inadequate to help someone lying in a ditch, holding on for dear life. But in reality such a rescue doesn't always require a Herculean effort.

St. Augustine once said, "Save by the grace of God, there go I" as he looked out at the sinners gathered in the court below. That's the absolute truth. If God's grace wasn't in your life right now, instead of reading this book you might be sleeping on a park bench, sipping on some crazy cocktail, or dealing with severe sexual problems. God's grace in your life has allowed you to make some good choices, as well as some poor ones.

If you're interested in using God's M.O. when you're confronted with hard choices, read on. If you find a quiet longing in your spirit calling for something more from life, read on. If you long for the world to stop calling Christians hypocrites, read on. If you want to help someone out of a ditch, read on.

The journey won't be easy. Some days it may require you walk down in a ditch and help someone who smells bad. You may get your hands dirty. Your clothes may get a little stained. You may risk your reputation. You may cause other people to question your choice in friends. But it's time for people who call themselves Christians to stop walking past others who are suffering on the side of the road.

Don't let fear force you into self-preservation mode. Don't let the world make you overly concerned about your own wants and needs. Think for a moment. Take a journey to discover God's M.O.

I'm confident this generation can rise up and initiate a social revolution. But for that to happen, we have to stop thinking about ourselves and start reaching out to people on the side of the road who want a friend instead of a judge. (Check out Romans 12:2-3.)

What if you looked at the world through new eyes? What if you had the opportunity to visit people lying in the ditch? Would you take any action, or would you walk on by? Let's take a walk together in your mind's eye.

The only ground rule is this: Be real. Don't walk down this dusty road if you're not ready to at least think about helping. Walk this journey to grow in your relationship with God. Walk this journey to learn. Walk this journey to examine your heart in order to find

God's truth in dealing with other people. A lot of people are lying in the ditches. They're crying out. They need help. They want you to put your arm around them. They want you to LOVE THIS!

/// CHAPTER 2 ///

GOD'S MOTIVE—LOVE

"AND SO WE KNOW AND RELY ON THE LOVE GOD HAS FOR US. GOD IS LOVE. WHOEVER LIVES IN LOVE LIVES IN GOD, AND GOD IN HIM. IN THIS WAY, LOVE IS MADE COMPLETE AMONG US SO THAT WE WILL HAVE CONFIDENCE ON THE DAY OF JUDGMENT, BECAUSE IN THIS WORLD WE ARE LIKE HIM. THERE IS NO FEAR IN LOVE. BUT PERFECT LOVE DRIVES OUT FEAR, BECAUSE FEAR HAS TO DO WITH PUNISHMENT. THE ONE WHO FEARS IS NOT MADE PERFECT IN LOVE." (1 JOHN 4:16-18)

The parable of the Good Samaritan is a good indication of how Jesus wants his followers to love people—even if we have very little in common with those people. In John 4:1-26 Jesus has an encounter that indicates just how deep our love should flow.

While in a Samaritan town called Sychar, Jesus stopped at a well where a local woman was drawing water. "Will you give me a drink?" he asked her.

The woman was shocked. The idea of a Jewish man talking to a Samaritan woman was so culturally out of bounds, she barely knew what to say. Here's how the conversation played out, according to Scripture:

> The Samaritan woman said to him, "You are a Jew and I am a Samaritan woman. How can you ask me for a drink?"

> Jesus answered her, "If you knew the gift of God and who it is that asks you for a drink, you would have asked him and he would have given you living water."

> "Sir," the woman said, "you have nothing to draw with and the well is deep. Where can you get this living water? Are you greater than our father Jacob, who gave us the well and drank from it himself, as did also his sons and his flocks and herds?"

> Jesus answered, "Everyone who drinks this water will be thirsty again, but whoever drinks the water I give him will never thirst. Indeed, the water I give him will become in him a spring of water welling up to eternal life."

> The woman said to him, "Sir, give me this water so that I won't get thirsty and have to keep coming here to draw water."

> He told her, "Go, call your husband and come back."

> "I have no husband," she replied.

Jesus said to her, "You are right when you say you have no husband. The fact is, you have had five husbands, and the man you now have is not your husband. What you have just said is quite true."

This is a life-changing story, not just for the Samaritan woman but for all followers of Jesus. In it Jesus shows us how to love unloved people.

One fell swoop to abolish racism

Notice that Jesus took a walk through Samaria, something Jews never did because of violent separatism in the culture. As I mentioned in chapter one, Samaritans were half-blooded people. The Assyrian invaders who had occupied Israel took wives and began producing mixed-race children. In response the Jews ostracized the half-breeds, believing they were only half-pure before God.

When Jesus took time out of his day to sit with someone of such an "impure" lineage, he brought attention to the absurdity of racism. When Jesus looked at people, he didn't see skin color or nationality or ethnic background. He saw their need for love. Check the New Testament, and you'll find that Jesus gave his time to all groups of people.

One fell swoop to affirm women

Jesus showed men how to love women, not in a sexual way but in a spiritual way—a practical way. In the New Testament culture of the Middle East, women were considered to be little more than servants to men.

Jesus, by sitting and talking with a Samaritan woman, began validating women as equals of men.

His attitude was nothing short of revolutionary. From his friendship with Mary and Martha to his healing of Peter's mother-in-law to his first post-resurrection appearance, Jesus left no doubt that women were a central part of his ministry—and key figures in spreading his gospel.

One fell swoop to advocate forgiveness

The woman Jesus approached had been married five times. What's more, she was living with a man who wasn't her husband at all. Jesus certainly knew about her sin of adultery, but it didn't stop his relentless pursuit to help her in times of need. Jesus didn't judge her before she had the ability to choose truth. He saw her need and helped her reach the object of her desire.

JESUS' MOTIVE: LOVE

Jesus was a revolutionary. He looked deep into the hearts of sinful people and, without a hint of judgment, offered them compassion and help in their times of need. If you're serious about following Jesus' example, you need to learn to demonstrate love to others in a meaningful way.

How, you ask?

Walk with me down a long, dusty road. Let's see if we can find people like the Samaritan woman, longing for needs to be met.

The homeless

Our first stop is an inner-city park where you notice people sitting by fountains, lying on park benches, and playing on merry-go-rounds. You spot a group of people huddled together around an old oil barrel. They've started a fire for heat. While they're warming their hands, others are holding cardboard signs at the corners of busy intersections, begging for food, longing for one person to stop and offer help. They all look like they've been here awhile. With their tattered clothes, long beards, and oily hair, they resemble an indigenous tribe from the Amazon jungle.

You watch as BMWs whiz past them. Out of nowhere a large SUV speeds up, the driver pretending to try to hit the group. Some of the homeless people fall as they scramble to get out of its way. The truck drives off with its blinker flashing as if to say, "Don't be here the next time, or I'll do it."

One man reaches down to help the fallen to their feet. He seems to be the leader. At the very least he's the most compassionate one of the bunch. After a couple of minutes you realize all the man really wants to do is support his family. He isn't a con man. He just wants some food for his family, a little love from someone who cares, and maybe just a little encouragement. What he gets is an occasional dollar bill, countless obscene gestures, and a variety of curse words from inside the cars that zoom past his corner.

With tattoos on his arms and a deep, dark, empty look on his face, it's obvious that his dignity is long gone. He'll settle for anything. He's just trying to make it one day at a time. He hasn't showered for weeks. He smells of the street. His breath makes people turn away in disgust. His clothes haven't been washed in ages.

You approach him with great caution. Your heart tells you to help, but your head reminds you of all the nightly news stories about violent attacks by homeless people.

Still, you are determined. You strike up a conversation with him. He tells you about his life before he became homeless. He mentions a wife, two kids, and a beautiful home he lost in one bad business deal. According to him, his situation isn't his fault. Corporate America was downsizing, and he got caught in the middle. He tells you his wife lives on the corner down the street, and his kids play on the playground behind you. They run around every day in the same old clothes, not knowing that anything's wrong. Over and over again he says, "We're so lucky to have each other." You look at the way he lives and wonder, "How can you call yourself lucky? You have nothing."

There are no worldly possessions in sight. He says he had a shopping cart, but yesterday someone stole it. Today he has nothing. A bench across town is his bed. Tomorrow he's thinking about hopping a Greyhound bus to find work in another city. He doesn't want to leave his family, but it might be the only hope they have to survive.

You have a new pair of shoes. You've got some new school clothes your parents bought for you about a week ago. You've got an iPod in your pocket, but you're hesitant to pull it out, knowing it cost more money than the guy will see in the next month. Your car is in the garage at home. You just got a new job at the local grocery store. Your future is looking good. You're going to have money in your pocket as soon as payday comes around.

How do you feel? What will you do? Will you help him, or walk away? I don't blame you for not wanting to see people who live like this. But the fact is, they can be found in almost every city or town in America. In the richest country of the world 1.4 million children are homeless. And we don't know how to help them. We don't know what to do. We go on living in big houses, driving fast cars, and vacationing in nice places. What else *can* you do? How are you supposed to help people who are so far gone?

Do you throw a five-dollar bill his way and wish him well? Do you spit and jeer like the hundreds of other drivers who pass by every day? Do you breathe a sigh of relief because you're glad it's not you? Do you invite him to church? Do you take him to a local fast food joint for a quick meal? Do you worry about what will happen if you let him in your car? Do you stare in disbelief? What do you do?

The homosexual

I have something else I want to show you just ahead, where the road enters that cultural hot spot—the one that offers all the amenities of modern technology. Here the road is called Tolerance Lane, and it's frequented by people who consider themselves "alternative."

When you walk down this road, you notice men holding hands. You see women with their arms around each other, not like friends but like something more. You notice people walking with a swagger that emphatically brands their alternate way of living.

You hear some kids shouting words like, "Queen!", "Dyke!", and "Fairy!" You see protestors holding signs that say, "God hates fags." Some are trying to start fights with the pedestrians on the road.

The locals say traffic on this road is getting worse each year. Television producers exploit the scene by using it as a backdrop for their shows. Movies glorify the lifestyles on display here. The school down the block teaches the importance of diversity and tolerance in an effort to change the mentality of the students. The new generation will look down this road with empathy, compassion, and no judgment of right and wrong.

Obviously, this is a different road from what you might have traveled before, but I guarantee you will walk it someday. How will you handle it? Will you damn these people to hell for sinning against a holy God? Will you dismiss the whole scene as being a matter of personal preference? Would you ever entertain the notion of having gay friends? If so, how would you interact with them? Would you invite them to your church? Would you be embarrassed to be seen with them?

The addict

Before we head back home, I've got one more place I want you to see. It's my apartment building. I unlock the outer gate and lead you down a narrow hallway. The familiar smell of pepperoni pizza fills the air as you walk past apartment 6A.

Next door you can hear the faint sounds of a familiar song. "Baby, don't worry...about a thing...every little thing...is gonna be all right." It's the rich reggae rumble of Bob Marley. You walk close to the door to listen carefully. You notice a funky smoke creeping out from the bottom of the door. You know the smell.

It's the same odor you smelled at your best friend's 16th birthday bash when you went to the restroom down the hall. You knocked on the door and thought it was strange that the door was locked because you could hear people talking inside. You were about to walk away when you heard the toilet flush and people start laughing. The door opened, and out came five or six guys on the football team, all of them laughing. They filed out, but the smell lingered. This is the same smell.

A little further down the hall, a doorway is cracked open. You stop to peer in. You notice two legs crossed on the edge of a couch. The television is on, and the volume is extremely loud. You knock on the door to make sure everything is okay. You see a young woman with a small pipe in one hand and a lighter in the other. She lights a small bulb on the end of the pipe and inhales deeply. She looks at you with a dull stare.

What do you do? How do you handle the situation? How do you approach someone strung out on drugs? What would you say if it were your friend in that apartment? Would you walk away? Would you pretend you didn't see anything? Would you invite her to church? Or would you be too embarrassed to be seen with her? Could you tell her about God's love, or do you think God has better things to do with his time?

These aren't easy scenes to witness. Society teaches us not to look—at least not with any compassion. Every day the world asks, "Why would you help someone who isn't going to help you?"

The answer is simple. You are not of the world. "If you belonged to the world, it would love you as its own. As it is, you do not belong to the world, but I have chosen you out of the world. That is why the world hates you" (John 15:19). Jesus makes it crystal clear that the world isn't going to recognize the love you have for other people because the world didn't recognize his love.

BANNERS OF IDENTITY

If you've ever been to a college football game, you know the key element of the experience—even more

than tailgating—is identification with the team. Some people wear jerseys. Some people sport hats, flags, or stickers. Some people drive cars painted with their team's colors. Almost everyone who attends has some "banner of identity" that brands him or her as a fan.

Along those same lines, there are banners that brand Christians as "fans" (or followers) of Christ. That is, certain truths need to be evident in our lives for everyone to see.

Banner #1: God's love is lavish.

"How great is the love the Father has lavished on us, that we should be called children of God! And that is what we are! The reason the world does not know us is that it did not know him." (1 John 3:1)

God's love is lavish. In fact, your very existence can be credited to a God who created you out of love. He made you special (Genesis 1:26). He created you from nothing and set you apart from the plants and animals. He made you the culmination of all creation. He desires the best for you because he created you to experience the best life has to offer.

He even knew you before you were born. The Bible says he knit you in your mother's womb (Psalm 139:13). He made your heart beat. He started your brain waves firing. He gave you muscles and created your personality before you came into the world.

He didn't create you to condemn you. He didn't create you for judgment. He didn't create you to make bad decisions and live in sin. But he accounted for that possibility. He provided for you from the beginning of time.

But that's only the tip of his love. When sin threatened to keep you apart from him for eternity, he made the ultimate sacrifice to prevent that from happening. He sent his only Son—one who was perfect, completely innocent of sin—to endure the punishment you deserve for your sin. God allowed his Son to be tortured and murdered for something you did.

And guess what! He didn't just do it for you. He did it for the whole of humanity. He did it for the kid sitting alone in the corner of the cafeteria. He did it for your next-door neighbor. He did it for the girl addicted to drugs. He did it for the guy caught in a homosexual lifestyle. He did it for the prostitute on the corner. The Bible says, "For God so loved the WORLD" (John 3:16).

So as we look at the motive and character of God, it's important to see the banner of his lavish love hanging over humanity. He loves, and for us to know him, we need to love, too.

Banner #2: God's love culminated in Jesus' life.

Many people believe in an aloof God, one who created the universe and then left it to its own devices. They believe that he's still out there somewhere but that he has little interest or involvement in our everyday lives.

If that were the case—if God really were an aloof, distant deity—there would be no reason for this book. If the Creator didn't care about other people, there would be no reason for us to care about them, either. There would be no reason to think about anyone but ourselves.

However, we believe in God Jehovah—the One who sent his Son to die on the cross—so we have an actual model of God's love. A living, breathing model who walked the earth 2,000 years ago.

Regarding that model, Jesus, the apostle Paul wrote, "He is the image of the invisible God, the first-born over all creation" (Colossians 1:15). If Jesus is the image of the invisible God, it makes sense to survey his actions here on earth to discover God's will for us on this planet. And if Jesus is the image of God the Father, then we can be imitators of God by imitating Jesus. Got that?

Jesus said, "As the Father has loved me, so have I loved you. Now remain in my love. If you obey my commands, you will remain in my love, just as I have obeyed my Father's commands and remain in his love. I have told you this so that my joy may be in you and that your joy may be complete. My command is this: Love each other as I have loved you. Greater love has no one than this, that he lay down his life for his friends" (John 15:9-13).

Jesus loves those who follow him. But he didn't limit his love to those who served in his ministry. Jesus showed genuine compassion to all people. He healed a man with leprosy (Matthew 8:2-4). He cast demons out of possessed people (Luke 9:38-43). He raised folks from the dead (Luke 7:11-17).

Jesus helped people inside his circle of friends and outside his sphere of influence. He modeled what it means to see beyond the needs of self, to look into the hearts of others. He recognized people's needs and dealt with them in ways that made those people feel loved and cared for. Keep in mind, too, that Jesus performed miracles for sinners. He didn't require people to be holy to receive his help.

When Jesus was asked what the greatest commandment in all of Scripture is, he replied, "'Love the Lord your God with all your heart and with all your soul and with all your mind.' This is the first and greatest commandment. And the second is like it: 'Love your neighbor as yourself.' All the Law and the Prophets hang on these two commandments" (Matthew 22:37-40).

If those are the two most important instructions in Scripture, Christians need to evaluate every decision, every action, and every thought in light of those commands. If I am supposed to love God with everything inside me, then all my actions need to be filtered through that commandment. And if I'm supposed to love my neighbor as myself, I need to figure out who my neighbor is.

Banner #3: God loves neighbors.

Five thousand men and several thousand women gathered near a hillside to hear Jesus speak. The crowd

was one of the largest of Jesus' earthly ministry. The people listened intently to his every word, hoping for something that would change their lives. Little did they know what lay in store for them.

After Jesus finished speaking, his disciples suggested that he adjourn the meeting and send the people into the surrounding towns to find food to eat. After all, the hour was getting late and the people were getting hungry.

Jesus had a better idea. He told his disciples to provide the food. They must have thought he was joking. Feeding a crowd of that size would have cost five months' wages at least. All they had was five loaves of bread and two fish.

Can you picture the scene? Jesus probably rolled his eyes at his disciples' lack of vision and faith before he instructed them to bring him the bread and fish. Quickly and efficiently, he multiplied the supplies on hand until everyone in the crowd had his or her fill. Afterward the leftovers filled 12 baskets (see Matthew 14:13-21).

Jesus wasn't concerned about the financial bottom line of his ministry. He didn't collect money for expenses from his followers. He didn't require people to join some "Holy Fellowship of Jesus Believers." He met people's needs with no strings attached. He loved his neighbors.

Who are your neighbors? Let me offer you a few hints. Some of them are white and some are black.

Some are short and some are tall. Some are overweight and some are thin. Everyone in your sphere of influence, everyone you encounter today, and everyone you ever encounter who has needs are your neighbors. It's not your job to discriminate between those who will receive your love and those who won't. Sometimes God puts people in your life who are hard to love. But you still have to love them. It's not your business to decide who receives your grace. Your job is to love your neighbor as you love yourself.

To answer the question, "How?" I invite you on a journey beyond your normal comfort boundaries. As you thumb through the chapters of this book, you are going to encounter several groups of people who are crying out for love. They don't need patronizing; they need neighbors who truly care for them. As you read, leave your preconceived notions behind. Open your mind to the possibilities of what will happen when God's people race to reach out to those who have long been discarded. Love them not for what they do but because God loves them. Introduce them to the loving Jesus who will be their key to the gates of heaven. Come along and LOVE THIS!

/// CHAPTER 3 ///

LOVING THE HOMELESS

"Come to me, all you who are weary and burdened, and I will give you rest. Take my yoke upon you and learn from me, for I am gentle and humble in heart, and you will find rest for your souls. For my yoke is easy and my burden is light." (Matthew 11:28-30)

He was holding a sign: "WILL WORK FOR FOOD." He had long hair and a shaggy beard. His clothes reeked of body odor. He probably hadn't showered in a week or more. His breath smelled of alcohol. Cigarette smoke hovered over the shopping cart that contained every worldly possession he owned.

Jerry was down on his luck. He had risen to success in the corporate world but now was nothing more than a homeless guy holding a sign. He had a family but was divorced. His two kids hated him. His wife had run off with another man. He got fired from his job. Now he moved from town to town like a migrant gypsy. He didn't know where he was going each day. He didn't

know where he would sleep each night. He didn't know where his next meal was coming from.

Hour after long hour he stood holding his sign as cars passed by. Drivers in Mercedes, Porsches, and BMWs all hurried past him on their way to do whatever it was they needed to do, ignoring the man who simply wanted some food. To them he didn't even exist. On this day Jerry waited patiently, knowing eventually someone would give him enough cash for a meal. And sure enough, someone did.

My friend Thomas has passion. His passion spreads from music to art to social responsibility. He longs to share Jesus with people who are down on their luck. And on this day he was going to get a chance to do just that.

Thomas was driving home from work in his beat-up pickup truck. Thomas loves to work. That's why he has two jobs—one at a fast food diner and the other at a local coffee shop. On first glance you might mistake Thomas for a street gypsy, but he is a solid family man. He has tattoos all over his body and piercings in the weirdest places, but he also has the cutest kid I've ever seen. His cough reveals years of smoking, and he colors his hair with different dyes, but he has one of the coolest wives I've ever been around. He's a living embodiment of the old saying, "Don't judge a book by its cover."

Thomas stopped at a red light and noticed Jerry holding his sign. He rolled down the window and asked Jerry if he needed a little help. When he opened the

car door, Jerry's eyes lit up. He grabbed a few items from his shopping cart and headed toward the truck.

Thomas could tell that Jerry needed food—that he wasn't looking for money for booze or drugs. He told Jerry to throw his stuff in the back of the truck, and together they headed for the diner where Thomas was the head grill man. Jerry broke down in tears and started telling Thomas his whole story.

Three months earlier Jerry's wife had decided she didn't love him anymore. She'd found another man and had been having an affair with him for a few weeks. She told Jerry he needed to move out so the new guy could move in. Jerry was crushed. "Where did the love go?" he wondered. "What happened to 'till death do us part'?"

Later that week Jerry's boss came to him and explained that the company was moving in a different direction and that Jerry's services were no longer needed. Jerry was laid off. Just when he thought things couldn't get any worse, they did.

Jerry's kids decided to side with their mother. Rather than sympathizing with their father after he lost his job, they rejected him. They called him names and told him he was worthless as a father.

That was the last straw as far as Jerry was concerned. So he walked away. He went to the local Greyhound station, bought a ticket to San Francisco, and left without saying goodbye. For reasons he can't fully

explain, he got off the bus in Waco, Texas, and decided to live under a bridge.

Inside the diner Thomas introduced Jerry as his new friend. At first Jerry didn't understand the introduction. After all, he had only just met Thomas. But he politely smiled as he shook everybody's hand. Then he took a seat in a booth next to the window. Thomas quickly placed an order for two sourdough hamburgers and then joined his new friend. He knew the window for sharing Jesus' love was small, and he didn't want to miss the opportunity.

"Why are you doing this?" Jerry asked.

"Doing what?" Thomas smiled.

"You stopped and invited me into your truck, you brought me to your work, and you bought my lunch. Why didn't you just throw money out the window like everyone else? Why do you want to help me?"

This was precisely the moment Thomas was hoping for, but he knew it was too soon. He resisted the temptation to evangelize and said simply, "Jerry, we all get to a point in life where we are down on our luck. Sometimes all we need is a friend." Jerry looked away when he couldn't hide the tears falling from the corners of his eyes.

Thomas has figured it out. He isn't compelled to look like a Christian; he's motivated to act as Jesus acted. Not all of us are cut out to get tattoos and piercings, but for Thomas these provide a way to tell migrant people that he's one of them—that Jesus cares, regardless of what we look like.

ISN'T THAT WHAT JESUS DID?

I remember singing the Sunday school song "Zacchaeus was a wee little man, and a wee little man was he. He climbed up in a sycamore tree for the Lord he wanted to see." If you're familiar with Zacchaeus' story, you know he was a crooked tax collector, a man despised by society. The Bible doesn't tell us what need drove Zacchaeus up the tree that day, but it does tell us how Jesus responded to him. Luke 19:5 says, "When Jesus reached the spot, he looked up and said to him, 'Zacchaeus, come down immediately. I must stay at your house today.'"

Imagine being Zacchaeus. You've seen crowds teem around Jesus, and all you want to do is get a good look at what's going on. You've heard that Jesus offers hope to people, but you know your chances of catching his attention are slim to none. Such is the fate of a short outcast of society.

So you climb a tree to catch a glimpse of the One who calls himself the Son of Man. And then it happens. Jesus singles you out and calls you by name. He tells you he wants to spend time with you. He invites himself to your house for the day. Imagine your joy and excitement!

The crowd's reaction to Jesus' plan is quick and severe. They complain about his choice of companions.

They fret about the fact that Jesus would consent to being the guest of a sinner. But Jesus doesn't let their short-sightedness stop him.

And that's where he and I differ. I know I have what someone else needs, but the mere fact that people might mutter and grumble about my getting involved often keeps me from doing the right thing. How many times have I driven past the guy holding the sign? How many Thanksgivings have I filled my belly while someone in my city is going hungry? How many times have I laid my head on my pillow in my comfortable bed while people are sleeping on park benches around the country? I'm ashamed, but I want to be honest with you. Why do I do that? Why do I allow other people's opinions to dictate my behavior? I want to be like my friend Thomas—and I think I can. All it takes is a little observation and a willingness to do something.

THE IMPORTANCE OF AWARENESS

Each summer I hire about 200 students to help run our camp in Kanakuk, Colorado. They come from colleges all over the country, and without a doubt they are among the most incredible people on the planet. They work hard. They play hard. And most of all, they love Jesus with all their hearts.

One summer I hired a counselor named Jarod. The picture he included on his application showed him hanging by a rope from a cliff, wearing a helmet that read, "EAT MORE BEEF." The first time I saw the picture I laughed out loud and thought, "This guy is pretty gutsy to put this kind of picture on the application." So I called him for an interview and ended up hiring him.

Jarod worked on the dock that first summer, driving boats and setting the sails for kids who wanted to sail on our little mountain lake. Though he was often exhausted at the end of the day, Jarod enjoyed the work. He turned out to be a loyal employee who needed a little encouragement and a whole lot of mentoring. Over time we became great friends.

Jarod worked for me for two years after he graduated high school. One evening as we sat on my porch, he started talking about some of the things he wanted to do in the future. He wanted to expand our rock program, start a climbing school, and perhaps even move to Colorado to live year-round.

I looked at him and said, "Sorry, pal, you're not working here next year."

Taken aback, he asked, "What do you mean?"

I said, "You have no college education, no formal job training. If you want to go anywhere in life, you need to go to school."

"I don't have any money!" he pointed out.

And he was right. He lived at the camp. I didn't pay him much other than room and board. He was "homeless" in a very different sense of the word.

"I'll tell you what," I said. "There is a college in my hometown that lets you have free tuition as long as you work a certain number of hours. I have a house with an extra bedroom. You apply to school, stay in my house, and then we'll think about next year."

Three years later Jarod is on the brink of graduating from college, applying to graduate schools, and getting his life on track.

Helping the homeless doesn't always mean buying a meal for the dirty guy on the street or taking someone to a shelter. Sometimes it means just BEING AWARE OF PEOPLE AROUND YOU. Sure, we need people to feed the homeless, but if there are no homeless people around, take a look at your friends and acquaintances and try to meet their needs.

Thomas is a master at meeting needs. He knew Jerry needed food, a physical need. But he also knew the importance of following up physical needs with spiritual mentorship.

While I was in college, I watched Thomas invite several homeless men to his diner. He would feed them, begin a friendship, and then invite them to his church to hear about the true bread of life.

The place was called The Church Under the Bridge, and it was awesome. Every Sunday morning the staff would set up a small sound system under the overpass of a major interstate. And every Sunday 50 to 75 homeless people would show up to see what was going on. Instead of passing around an offering plate to get money, the staff passed around boxes of cigarettes to communicate the fact that they were there to give and not take.

As you might imagine, I was a little uneasy about a church giving out cigarettes. But most of the people who attended were hooked on nicotine. And once they became part of the church, the church offered programs designed to help them stop smoking. But for the time being, the church wanted to help with their *immediate* needs. The staffers weren't looking for anything in return other than an open heart and a willingness to listen to the gospel.

Each Sunday the pastor gave a clear gospel presentation. Usually, at least one or two folks in the audience would accept Jesus into their lives, and the journey to discipleship would begin. They began longing for spiritual food, and the church filled them up. It was an amazing concept.

Until that point in my life, I had never seen a homeless person. I heard horror stories of violent criminals living on the street. I had been told that many homeless people actually made more money than most hardworking citizens because they didn't pay taxes. My attitude toward the homeless at that time was, "I have to work, so you should, too. Get off your lazy behind and go get a job." (It's no wonder the world has so much contempt for Christians.)

But The Church Under the Bridge changed all that. In the most unassuming place on the planet I saw people emulating Jesus' call. They weren't concerned about their budget. They didn't put a lot of thought into the songs they sang. They didn't have a baptismal. They didn't have stained glass windows. In fact, they didn't even have chairs for several years.

What they had was the desire to reach out to the lowest socioeconomic group in America and validate those people as human beings. If you don't think that will get someone's attention, you should go watch it. Go watch someone with no hope suddenly get hope. Go watch someone with no food suddenly get food. Better yet, take an active role in the process. Find someone who doesn't have the slightest idea where his next meal, his next dollar, or even his next "Hey, how are you doing?" is coming from and meet his need. Say hi. Slip a dollar in his pocket. Or take some food to him and spend the afternoon in a conversation that ignites a fire in a cold, dark soul.

When was the last time you helped a homeless man or woman? Have you been to the city to pass out blankets or coats to people who sleep under the stars every night? Have you taken time to help feed those who are down on their luck?

I've often wondered why churches aren't filled with homeless people. Is it because members object to the smell of the homeless? Does it have to do with their clothes or hair or scraggly beards? Have we convinced ourselves that church is a place for people who dress right and act right?

I hope not.

LOVE THIS!

Jesus had words for people like that. "Woe to you, teachers of the law and Pharisees, you hypocrites! You are like whitewashed tombs, which look beautiful on the outside but on the inside are full of dead men's bones and everything unclean. In the same way, on the outside you appear to people as righteous but on the inside you are full of hypocrisy and wickedness" (Matthew 23:27-28). Jesus saw the Pharisees parading around in their religious attire, saying the right words, and acting the right way. But he knew they were dead inside. They didn't care about people. They cared only about their position in society and their position in heaven.

In college those whitewashed tombs lived right down the hall in my dorm. I went to a large southern Christian university. A place where it was cool to be a Christian. A place where getting dressed up and going to church was the right thing to do.

One particular Sunday morning, though, after a Saturday night had gotten a little late, I decided to attend the local "Bedside Baptist Church." (For those of you unfamiliar with the term…I slept in.) Around 11:30 a.m. I finally stumbled out of my room and made my way to the bathroom. There I saw my friend, who had also visited Bedside Baptist that morning. But he was putting on a three-piece suit so that when he went to the cafeteria, it would look as though he had gone to church that morning.

I remember thinking, "Are you kidding me? Is this what faith has become? A group of people who are concerned about presenting themselves as holy without giving any thought to being 'real' in front of other people?"

AN INESCAPABLE PRECEDENT

If you really want to develop the proper mindset for ministering to the homeless, take a minute to think about what God did for us. He left his exalted position in heaven to come to our place of dwelling. He left the angels who offered him nonstop praise and adoration. He left the streets of gold. He set aside his power and glory to die on a cross for us. That's how much he loved us.

I wonder if we smelled funny to him. I wonder if our clothes looked shabby compared to heavenly attire. I wonder how much of an inconvenience it was for the king of the universe to be born in a lowly manger.

Of course, none of that mattered to Jesus. All that mattered to him is that we needed help—and that we had nowhere else to turn. That's what brought him to a place where the people were considerably less appealing than the ones he was used to and where the surroundings were much less pleasant. He reached out to us so that we could know him and enjoy the life he offers.

Shouldn't we do the same for our friends living on the street? We Christians need to help to alleviate the homeless problem in America. We Christians need to feed the hungry in America. We have the numbers to accomplish the task. Here's how.

1. Find the homeless in your community.

Some cities have people sleeping on the street; others have people sleeping in shelters. Call the Salvation Army, the Church Army, or the Red Cross and ask how you can help today. The only way to help the homeless is to *find the homeless.*

2. Figure out the need and meet it.

Some people need food. Others need water. Some people need shelter. Others need clothes. Some people need money. Others just need a friend. Zacchaeus needed a friend, and Jesus met his need. He went to Zacchaeus' house and, by being a friend, helped him see his need for forgiveness. You can do the same thing.

If organizations need helpers, volunteer for an hour a week. If they need clothes, start a clothing drive. Knock on every door in your neighborhood and ask for old clothes your neighbors don't need anymore. If it's food they need, contact local grocery stores to see if you can get the leftovers. There are countless ways to help. We just have to FIGURE OUT THE NEED AND MEET IT!

3. Feed people the Spirit.

I think the coolest part of Jesus' ministry is that he was able to meet physical needs and then follow up with spiritual wisdom. Gone are the days when you could walk down the street with a "Four Spiritual Laws" tract in your back pocket. People just don't respond to that approach anymore. But if you address people's physical needs, you might have an opportunity, like Thomas did, to answer the question, "Why are you doing this?"

I can't think of a question that honors Christ more. Why would you help someone you don't know—someone you may never see again? Why would you take time out of your busy schedule to help someone who has no intention of helping you? Could it be that you are living a life worthy of your faith?

I challenge you today: Go find someone in need. Sacrifice your time and money to show that person how much God loves him or her. Remember what Jesus said: "Whatever you did for the least of these...you did for me" (Matthew 25:40).

/// CHAPTER 4 ///

LOVING THE HOMOSEXUAL

He swaggered into the theater, announcing with a heavy lisp, "I hope you guys have your eyes on another role because yours truly just gave the audition of a lifetime." Harrison Petty, a 30-year-old college sophomore, returning to complete a directing degree after five years in the Big Apple, had just finished his audition for the biggest show of the year.

One look at him and the stereotypical labels started flying through my mind—gay, homo, queer, fag. The kind of hurtful words you'd expect to come from uneducated homophobes. But in this case the words came from the mind of a believer. They came from someone who claimed to love God with all his heart. They came from a man devoted to loving other people. They came from me.

Not that Harrison would have been surprised to hear them. According to him, his journey as a homosexual started at age six. On the playground at recess he realized he had more interest in what the girls were doing than what the boys were doing. Later while the guys were playing football, Harrison was learning how to dance. While the boys were playing cowboys and Indians, Harrison was putting on dresses and accessorizing his latest fashion motif. There was no doubt in Harrison's mind that he was gay.

He graduated from high school in Ennis, Texas, and enrolled in the largest Baptist university in the world. Needless to say, he didn't fit in. Homosexuality before the 1980s was a taboo lifestyle. If you were gay, you were lost. You were lonely. No one tried to understand you.

The only comfort Harrison found was in the company of like-minded people. The world hated him. Christians ostracized him. After a couple of years at the Baptist university, he decided the hating had to stop. He was tired. Tired of believers yelling at him. Tired of faculty members dismissing him. Tired of friends leaving him. He picked up and moved to New York City in search of the bright lights, the big city, and most important, a community that would accept his alternative sexuality.

Harrison joined a dance troupe and performed for thousands while waiting for his big break. It never came. Hungry, tired, and longing for friendship, Harrison called an old mentor at the university, and she convinced him to move back and finish the degree he started long ago.

His return to in the local theater caused quite a stir. The largely conservative student body steered clear of the homosexual crowd. They closed their eyes and ears to the artistic community, hoping the "gay problem" would just go away. But Harrison was not going away. He was tired of stereotyping. He was tired of name-calling. He was tired of it all.

BEYOND STEREOTYPES

Harrison was unashamed and unapologetic about his sexuality. He had found confidence in New York, and he wasn't going to put up with discrimination any longer. He didn't go searching for a fight, and he didn't try to "convert" anyone. He just wanted people to understand that, as far as he was concerned, he had no choice in the matter. He believed he had been born gay and was simply living the life he'd been intended to live. He was honest with himself and with those around him. And that was the beginning of our friendship.

I love honesty—sometimes to a fault. I would rather people be honest about who they are, even if it means living in sin, than lie about who they are and pretend to be Christlike. Harrison was honest. Granted, I didn't agree with his lifestyle. But he certainly wasn't trying to impress or fool anyone. And I respected that.

One summer just after we came back from a three-month break, I knew something was wrong with Harrison. His zeal for life had been dulled by some kind of emotional turmoil. No one understood why he was sulking around, why he didn't have the normal pep to his step, why he seemed so serious.

One night after rehearsal Harrison asked me to give him a ride back to his apartment. I was surprised because he'd never asked me to take him home before. On the way he asked to pull over. I felt a little weird, but I pulled the car to the corner of the street. He looked at me and asked, "Andy, can I tell you something?"

"Sure," I said.

"This was the hardest summer of my life," he explained. "I got really sick at the beginning of June, and the doctors didn't know what to do or how to treat it. They decided I'd better go and get tested."

As the tears began to roll down his cheeks, he told me his HIV test had come back positive.

My initial reaction was embarrassing. "Am I being exposed to HIV right now?" I wondered. "Should I touch the car handle he used to get in? Should I avoid the bathrooms he uses? Can I get HIV from just talking to him?" This was the early 1990s, when doctors were still trying to figure out the modes of transmission for HIV. Back then HIV was a death sentence. There were no drug cocktails to keep people alive like the ones patients have today. If you were diagnosed as HIV-positive, it was time to go home and get your life in order.

But this was my friend, so my initial thoughts didn't linger. "Harrison, what can I do?" I asked.

"Nothing," he said. "I don't need to be a sympathy case. I don't need you to DO anything. What I need is a friend. I need someone I can count on. Can I count on you?"

"Sure, whatever I can be for you," I said.

I dropped Harrison off at his apartment and wept all the way home. The man I had once called a "fag" was now one of my closest friends. We laughed together. We cried together. We worked on our craft together. We fought together. In the end our relationship was more like a brotherhood than a friendship. All I could think about was that the theater wasn't going to be the same without Harrison.

The next year was hard. I watched my friend go from being the life of the party to a lifeless, hopeless human waiting to die. He was nauseated by the medicine he took. He lost his hair due to another disease. Every common cold was a potentially fatal virus for him.

Six months after he told me he was sick, Harrison died.

I don't know if I handled our friendship right. I don't know if I did everything in my power to tell Harrison about Jesus. I didn't give him a tract with the prayer of salvation on it. But I do know this: Harrison gave me a new perspective.

At first our relationship was marked by name-calling and immature insecurity. In the end I found a friend. And Harrison saw that all Christians aren't necessarily haters. I realized that all homosexuals aren't out to seduce others into having sex. He saw a man he once called "the breeder" turn from a bigot into a brother. I saw a hurting man who had been burned by religion healed by the lifestyle of one believer committed to a relationship with Christ—a relationship that involved loving others.

THE WORST SIN?

Homosexuality is one of those hard issues Christians have to come to terms with. The Bible is consistent from the Old Testament to the New Testament in stating that homosexual behavior is a sin. But rather than using that fact as a weapon against homosexuals, try looking at it from another perspective.

Do you know anyone who has ever told a lie? If so, do you still hang out with that person? When I was a kid I lied to my parents about taking gum from a grocery store. Though I may have been young at the time, I was still guilty of lying. That makes me a liar.

I've never cheated on my wife. But in Matthew 5:27-28 Jesus said, "You have heard that it was said, 'Do not commit adultery.' But I tell you that anyone who looks at a woman lustfully has already committed adultery with her in his heart." If any man reading this book is honest with himself, he, like me, would have to confess to committing adultery. So we are all adulterers.

Why, then, do many Christians accept some sins and reject others? Why have we created a "sin scale," on which some transgressions are considered more offensive to God than others? I can't answer those questions. But I do know that our attitude is hurtful. And I know that when some people look to Christianity, all they find is rejection.

The Bible deals with homosexuality in a few different places. 1 Corinthians 6:9-11 says, "Do you not know that the wicked will not inherit the kingdom of God? Do not be deceived: Neither the sexually immoral nor idolaters nor adulterers nor male prostitutes nor *homosexual offenders* nor thieves nor the greedy nor drunkards nor slanderers nor swindlers will inherit the kingdom of God."

While those verses certainly hit at the heart of the matter, we must not forget the rest of the passage: "And that is what some of you were. But you were washed, you were sanctified, you were justified in the name of the Lord Jesus Christ and by the Spirit of our God."

The Bible doesn't rank sins from 1 to 10 according to their relative badness. Instead Romans 3:23 says, "All have sinned and fall short of the glory of God." Homosexuals and heterosexuals alike fall into the category of the damned. It is only by God's grace and mercy that we are allowed to stand before him, reconciled.

Perhaps, then, we should reexamine the way we respond to people's sins. Perhaps instead of treating certain sins as more despicable than others, we should remind ourselves that we are all sinners, period. We all deserve eternal damnation. The fact that some of us are able to hide our sins better than others doesn't make us any less guilty in God's eyes.

So how does that apply to our interaction with homosexuals? How can we love people who live openly in a way God doesn't approve of? Here are some principles to consider.

1. Homosexuals are people.

Homosexuals are men and women trying to make their way through life the best way they know how. Just like everyone else, they are in the process of sorting out their issues, questioning their decisions, and working through their problems. In short, they are very much like you and me.

Christians need to stop treating homosexuality like the plague. We have done a terrible job figuring out how to love the gay community. My friend Harrison called Christians "haters." How in the world can you read the Bible from beginning to end, receive the ultimate grace and forgiveness of the Creator of the universe, and conclude that the ones who bought into that grace are haters? Take a look around. We give people like Harrison plenty of examples of hate.

Ask the men in your Christian community what they think about alternative lifestyles, and you'll likely hear

grumbles, complaints, and comments such as, "That's disgusting." (You can be sure that any homosexuals in the community hear those things, too.) Ask them about adultery and you'll likely hear the same things—that is, until they see a Hooters billboard on the way home. Suddenly adultery—the lusting with the eyes that Jesus warned about—may not seem like such a big deal.

Few Christians would reject a man who admitted to ogling sexy women. Why can't we extend the same courtesy to people who admit to preferring members of the same sex? Why do we treat homosexuals as though they're suffering from an incurable disease? Why can't we see them as people who struggle with sin, just as we do?

I had another theater friend named Mark. Mark's goal was to impress his fellow actors by bringing a new boy date to every party we threw. He was determined to bring new faces around just to prove he was gay, and he took pleasure in watching other people's reactions to his gayness. To be honest, his actions made me sick. I couldn't handle the way he put his sexuality on display. I was totally homophobic when I first met Mark. And, fortunately or unfortunately, it showed.

We had an audition in Mississippi for a Shakespeare festival, and the whole theater gang traveled together on a bus. When we pulled up to the hotel where we were staying, Mark yelled across the bus, "Is ANDY BRANER going to stay in the same hotel with US?" (meaning the gay fellas). Everybody on the bus laughed in disbelief. In response I looked straight in his eyes and said, "Why not?"

I spent four years trying to figure out how my faith could coexist with my interest in art. I spent countless hours seeking God's direction after my friend Harrison died. I realized that God doesn't hate gays; he hates sin. He hates the actions that keep us from experiencing the depth of his love. He hates that we ignore his directives. He hates that we are selfish. He hates that we lie. But he doesn't hate people.

How can he? He created us. He loved us and continues to love us to the very end. The Bible says, "Turn, O Lord, and deliver me; save me because of your unfailing love" (Psalm 6:4). God's love is never-ending. His love never fails. His love remains true, no matter what you do or when you do it. I was determined to communicate that truth.

"Why not?" I answered Mark in front of everyone. "Why not stay in the same hotel?"

An immediate hush fell over the bus. Mark's expression changed. In that instant he realized my friendship wasn't contingent on his being gay or not being gay. I was going to love Mark, even though I didn't agree with his sexual preference. I wanted to love him like God loves me. Like God loves him.

If you're serious about reaching out to homosexuals, you must look for opportunities to prove to the community that they are people just like you.

2. Homosexuals need acceptance.

One of the most difficult aspects of homosexuality is the fact that so many people who are struggling with their sexuality don't understand what's going on inside their heads. There are many theories as to why someone "becomes gay." Whether it's a matter of genetics or family dysfunction is a debate for another book. What we can agree on is that many homosexuals experience a lack of acceptance, both before and after they "come out."

Joe came to me a few years ago and confessed his struggle with homosexuality. In talking with Joe, I found out that Joe's father never said anything kind to Joe—ever. His father expected perfection in everything, from sports to academics. And he was relentless in his demands. Nothing was ever good enough for him. As a result Joe never got acceptance from the one person he needed it from most.

To complicate matters, Joe was quite effeminate. He liked art, painting, and theater. The kids on the playground called him "fag," "queer," and "girly man." After a while Joe began to wonder if they were right.

In college Joe finally found a group of people who accepted him for who he was. He began hanging out with the homosexual crowd. They brought him into their circle with no strings attached. He was so impressed by the nonjudgmental way his college friends treated him that more often than not, he would migrate to what they were doing—even if I was in town visiting.

It was a difficult four years, but I walked side by side with Joe. We talked about different books to read. We talked about the fact that God loved Joe in spite of his rebellion. We sought advice from some of the best sex counselors in the country. Finally, one day he told me, "Andy, I understand my problem. I've been running. Running from things I fear. Running to things I thought would provide security for me. My straight friends think I'm weird, but my gay friends accept me. My dad thinks I'm girly, but my gay friends think I'm cool. Maybe the issue isn't sexuality but identity and security. Maybe I need to spend some time working on my identity in Jesus and spend less time worrying about my identity in this world."

Joe found acceptance and learned that self-sacrificing love comes only from God. Today Joe is doing great. He's married and wants to have children someday.

3. Homosexuals are on the same journey we're on.

For me the hardest part in figuring out how to love the homosexual community was getting past stereotypes. However, once I became friends with some gay people, I realized that the human condition is consistent whether you're gay or straight. The fact is, we are all on a journey to find truth—but we all find it in different ways.

I also realized that God had placed me in the lives of several homosexual people who needed to know about life—specifically, the abundant life that only God offers. God gave me the opportunity, and I had

LOVE THIS!

a responsibility to take advantage of it. Ignoring that responsibility would have been disastrous.

Imagine you and I are hiking up a mountain in Colorado. It's a hot day, so on the way up, you take sip after sip from your water bottle. A couple hours into the hike, you put your bottle to your lips, only to discover it's empty. You have nothing to drink and no way to refill your bottle for several hours. Your throat is dry, and you start having trouble swallowing. You're thirstier than you've ever been in your life.

You look over at me and notice my water bottle is full. I pull it out and start chugging water so fast that it runs out the sides of my mouth and down my shirt. When I've had my fill, I pour the rest over my head, all the while talking about how refreshed I feel.

What would you think of me in that situation? You'd think I was a jerk, right? If I had a surplus of something you really needed but kept it to myself, you would have every right to call me a jerk.

Likewise, some Christians act like spiritual jerks in the way we relate (or don't relate) to the homosexual community. We have the wellspring of life inside us, but we neglect to share it with those who are most needy.

Not long ago I met a man named Bob who is working to educate pastors in Africa about the AIDS crisis on that continent. As one of the leading AIDS counselors in Africa, Bob has many resources to help pastors understand the emotional, spiritual, and physical nature of the AIDS epidemic as it relates to members of their congregations in Africa.

I told Bob about my friend Harrison and the experiences we went through while he was dying. I wept as I told the story. Bob kept an open ear while I worked through some hard memories. At the end of our conversation, he said, "Andy, I want you to know I have AIDS."

"What?" I asked.

"I've been living with AIDS for the last 17 years," he explained. "The Lord is using my life to minister to many people who are dealing with this crisis. I want you to know, you did the right thing. Loving your friend to his death is the very act of compassion Jesus spoke about when he said, 'Greater love has no one than this, that he lay down his life for his friends'" (John 15:13).

Laying down our lives doesn't necessarily mean dying for our friends. In some cases it might mean laying down our pride for them—or laying down our preconceptions. It might mean extending a hand of compassion, even if it's not popular with the "Christian" crowd. It might mean offering that bottle of water, even when it seems as if the other person isn't going to drink it.

My friendship with Harrison taught me how to love my neighbor better. It taught me that neighbors aren't necessarily the people I sit next to on Sunday morning. Sometimes they are people with different opinions, different experiences, and different outlooks on life.

LOVE THIS!

Some of my neighbors have worldviews I don't agree with. Some of them make lifestyle choices I don't agree with. That doesn't mean I should compromise my standards or change my beliefs to condone something the Bible speaks against. But it does mean I should look deep in my own heart at the sins I struggle with on a daily basis. That way, when I look around at other people, instead of condemning them for the lack of God's grace in their lives, I can conjure up the love and compassion Jesus commands me to give.

Echoing the most famous love chapter in the Bible, I say, "And now these three remain: faith, hope and love. But the greatest of these is love" (1 Corinthians 13:13).

/// CHAPTER 5 ///

LOVING THE ADDICTED

"I LIFT UP MY EYES TO THE HILLS—WHERE DOES MY HELP
COME FROM? MY HELP COMES FROM THE LORD, THE MAKER
OF HEAVEN AND EARTH." (PSALM 121:1-2)

J.T. was a typical teenager. He enjoyed hanging out with friends, going to the movies, and chillin' at the local skate park. He loved skating—something about the freedom, the rebellion, the attitude. He was totally into it. He spent hours and hours working on different skate moves with an eye toward entering a national skate competition in Denver, Colorado.

The grand prize was a deal with a major skating label, so J.T. worked hard. He saw skating as the only way out of his dead-end life. His mother worked long hours, and his father was an absentee parent. He'd met his dad a few times when he was little, but when his father remarried, J.T. was no longer a priority to him. J.T.'s mom was there for him as much as she could be.

She drove him downtown to the park where he could work on his skating and hang out with his friends. She picked him up when the sun went down and even provided a makeshift ambulance when J.T. or his friends got hurt. Hospital employees knew that anytime the tan and brown 1995 Chevy Suburban pulled up to the curb, there was likely some kind of emergency bone work to do.

J.T. and his skater "tribe" weren't fazed by injury. It only seemed to fuel their passion to get back on the rails and the pipes.

One afternoon some new guys came to the park. They landed moves J. T. and his tribe only dreamed of. As the newcomers pulled bigger and bigger tricks, J. T. wondered, "Where did these guys come from?"

After a while, he worked up the nerve to talk to them. "Hey, can you guys teach us how to do that stuff?" he asked.

"Yeah, bro, it's pretty easy," one of the guys replied. "Just a bowl and a prayer, and you're set for life."

"A bowl and a prayer? What's this guy talking about?" J.T. wondered. "Hey, where can a guy get that kind of bowl?" he asked.

"Come around in the morning, and I'll show you," the guy replied.

The next morning J.T. came to the park early. While he was throwing some tricks, his new mentor showed

LOVE THIS!

up with a smile on his face and a funny-looking tube in his hand. "Come on, bro," he said. "Let me show you the way to skater freedom."

He pulled a small bag out of his back pocket and fiddled briefly with a bowl, a tube, and a lighter. He put his lips around the mouth of the tube and inhaled smoke from the bowl. He held his breath in for a little bit and then passed the tube to J.T. "Go ahead, drag on this for a sec," he said.

J.T. put his mouth to the tube reluctantly, but he figured if this was the secret of great skating, he was willing to try it. The boys finished the bowl, picked up their boards, and started skating. J.T. couldn't feel anything, but he noticed everything seemed to move in slow motion. He jumped off the first ramp and hit the biggest air of his life. "WHOA! You're gonna have to get me some of that," he told his new friend.

"No problem, bro," his friend replied. "It'll set you free, man."

For the next five years J.T. was anything but free. He became addicted to weed. It became part of who he was. He smoked when he skated, when he was home watching TV, or when he just wanted to relax a little. His life revolved around dime bags, roaches, and bongs. And it all started because he wanted to skate better.

When I met J.T., he seemed like a normal kid, but he was lost in the world of recreational drugs. He didn't even know he needed help. As far as he was concerned, everything was okay in his world as long as he had weed. When J.T. came to our camp, he was surprised when we told him to get rid of his drug paraphernalia.

"Come on, man, it's only to help me cope," he begged as we threw his drugs in the toilet and pitched the pipe in the trash.

Over the next two weeks J.T. struggled with his craving for drugs, but he really wanted to be free of the hold drugs had on his mind and body. I can honestly say I've never been more proud of a kid in all my life. He made it to the end of the camp session, came up to me on the closing night, and threw his arms around my neck.

"Thank you for showing me what true love is," he said. "My friends didn't really love me. They just wanted to get high. Thanks for showing me what God's love is all about!"

It's a rewarding job to lead someone to freedom, and God hasn't stopped introducing me to people who are deep into the drug culture.

THE REAL TRUTH OF ADDICTION

Addiction is scary—scary for the addict and scary for those around him. Addiction literally controls the person in its grasp. It saps his spirit. It clouds his thinking. It causes him to do things he wouldn't normally do. It causes him to act in ways he wouldn't normally act.

Consider that a warning. If you're serious about showing love to someone who's struggling with addiction, you need to BE CAREFUL. An addict's world is a dangerous place. Drug deals go bad. Alcoholics get in fights. People who trip on acid do some crazy stuff. So you must always be aware of what's going on around you.

Once you've established a sense of self-preservation, then you can start loving, start encouraging, start reaching out to people. Jesus said, "Greater love has no one than this, that he lay down his life for his friends" (John 15:13). That doesn't mean Jesus is calling you to lay down your life for the coke addict across town, but he IS calling you to step out of your comfort zone and stop turning a blind eye to people who need help.

FREE AT LAST

Every year I organize conferences designed to help youth workers learn how to equip teenagers to deal with critical issues (such as the impact of the media or new philosophies being taught in school). I met Jean at one of those conferences. She sat in the front row, listening intently to every word and taking meticulous notes.

During a break I walked over to Jean's table and introduced myself. She told me she lived in the area and was interested in learning how to share the gospel with teenagers. Specifically, she wanted to know how to reach out to teenagers who were addicted to crystal meth. I was puzzled by her request. I'd never met a youth leader so focused on reaching such a specific audience.

"Why are you interested in helping kids on meth?" I asked.

Glancing at her husband, who was sitting next to her, she said, "Because we've been sober for about six months, and we feel that God allowed us to live so that we could teach kids about the loving compassion of Jesus."

I listened intently as she began telling her story.

"I was a full-fledged alcoholic by the age of 10," she explained. "My mother didn't have time to take care of me or play with me, so she used to get a beer out of the fridge, and I would drink it to quiet down. My parents didn't want to hear me cry, so every drink was fixed to get me buzzed. My grandmother thought it was funny when I stumbled around the kitchen, drunk."

I couldn't believe what I was hearing. Were there really families in the world that would let their 10-year-olds drink beer and then laugh because they were drunk?

"My family has a long history of drug addiction," she explained. "I was smoking cigarettes by the time I was eight."

"How did you get started on cigarettes?" I asked.

"My grandmother thought it was funny to watch me light her cigarettes. After lighting them over and over again, it became natural for me. She used to take pictures of me with a cigarette hanging out of my mouth. I started lighting my own when she was asleep in the back room. I taught myself how to inhale."

"Are you kidding me? You were an alcoholic and addicted to nicotine by the time you were 10?" I asked.

"That's not all," she said. "When I turned 13, my mother's boyfriend asked if I had ever smoked weed. I said no, and he offered me a hit of this huge joint he was carrying. It didn't really do anything to me for a little while, but the more I smoked, the better I felt. I smoked marijuana every day from when I was 14 until I turned 17."

"How did you get clean?" I asked. I knew several teenagers who were dealing with the same issue.

"Well, after weed didn't do anything for me anymore, a friend introduced me to acid," she explained. "I thought it was the greatest high, so for a couple of years, I would hit acid three or four times a week. My brain was going crazy. Hitting acid got old pretty quick, and my friend introduced me to another 'friend' who showed me how to cook my own meth. You don't know high like the high you get from doing meth. You feel invincible. You feel like you are on top of the world. Every sense in your body feels heightened to some sort of superhero status.

"My husband and I met while we were doing meth together in my aunt's trailer home," she continued. "We got married three months later. We kept on doing meth until about six months ago, when we had a car wreck. We were both high. It was rainy. We lost control of the car, and the next thing I knew, I was pulling him out, thinking I was on fire.

"The paramedics and firemen came to help us, and I was so high, I didn't feel a thing. My husband was knocked unconscious, but the only injury I had was a broken leg. We went to the hospital in the ambulance and were released the next day.

"Later I went to the car lot where they had taken the wreckage. When I saw what was left of the vehicle, I knew somebody or something was watching out for me that day. The front of the car was smashed all the way up to the dashboard. You could actually see the engine on the passenger's seat. The driver's seat wasn't accessible because the radiator was taking up the space where the seat was. It was a crazy, epiphany-type moment. I knew right then, God had sent a team of angels to protect us that night. There is no way I should have gotten out of the car and walked away. I went home and told my husband what I had seen. We knelt right there in the middle of the kitchen floor and prayed, 'God, if you can forgive a couple of drug bums like us, we'll serve you until we die. We want to know about you and the world we live in. Please forgive our sins. We want to do it right.'

"It was on that floor that I committed my life to serving teenagers. The drug problem here in America won't be changed by some government policy. Drug laws only inhibit people who obey the laws. Criminals will always be criminals and do stuff the law doesn't allow. I want to help the criminals. I want to help the victims of this meaningless addiction and introduce them to the saving power of Jesus. He is ultimate satisfaction, and I believe teens need to know it."

With that she sat back in her seat and smiled like someone who knew she'd been freed from the chains of slavery.

What a story! What conviction! I could actually sense the heart of Jesus in her as she spoke. And it occurred to me that if Jesus walked the planet today, he would likely be ministering to the same people Jean wanted to reach.

Think about it. He called the religious leaders of his day a "brood of vipers" (Matthew 3:7) and "whitewashed tombs" (Matthew 23:27), but he gave his time and compassion to tax collectors and prostitutes. Jesus' earthly mission was to meet the needs of people. People looking for assurance. People longing for satisfaction. People trying to fill deep voids in their lives. Jesus offered the only remedy that could fulfill every craving in the human soul: his love.

YOUR MOVE

If you're interested in helping people who are struggling with addiction discover Jesus' love, here are three things you can do.

1. Reach out.

You don't have to hide the fact that you are a Christian. You don't have to lurk in the shadows, embarrassed because you serve God. You have valuable help to offer, whether the world recognizes it or not.

Reach out to the kid sitting by himself at lunch. Reach out to the girl trying to hide her dependency on weed. Reach out to the drug addict who was taken to the hospital after another overdose. Take a little time to relate to kids you know who are interested in doing drugs. Don't run from them. Don't avoid them.

To reach addicts where they are, you'll likely have to step out of your comfort zone. You may find yourself doing things you never could have imagined—things like making sure someone who's high gets home safely. Or taking a friend to a rehab facility. Or holding someone accountable to stay out of her parents' liquor cabinet by regularly checking in with her. Who knows? Your efforts may save a friend from a fatal car wreck, a future broken marriage, or a wasted life.

Addicts need to know God's love like you know God's love. They need an opportunity to climb out of their despair. They need to know someone loves them and cares about their well-being. Will you be that someone? Will you schedule time each week to meet with a girl who's struggling with weed addiction? Will you take time to encourage someone who thinks alcohol is the answer? Will you listen to him, cry with him, celebrate progress with him, and help him see

LOVE THIS!

a future for himself? You may be surprised how far a little attention and a lot of love will go.

2. Consult professional help.

Many addicts are unable to overcome their addictions on their own. They need professional help—or at least help from someone with more experience and training than you have. Your community likely offers many programs for treating drug addiction and alcohol abuse. Learn all you can about them. Talk to your youth leader about your situation; get his input. Equip yourself with as much information as possible so that when the time is right, you can offer a helpful recommendation to an addicted friend. Once you've made the recommendation, you can periodically encourage your addicted friend to seek help.

3. Don't forget about them.

After you've reached out to an addict and encouraged him to seek professional help, your job is done, right? Wrong.

Helping someone battle an addiction is a marathon, not a sprint. The inner voices that drive people to drink or do drugs or seek out pornography don't go away after a day or week or even a month "on the wagon." That's why you need to be prepared to go the distance with an addict. Stay in contact. Maintain your accountability relationship. Regularly schedule times to get together and talk.

If your friend has setbacks on the road to recovery, stay in the battle. Most recovering alcoholics need people who don't judge them for a mistake, but rather are on the journey for the long haul. If your friend slips up, don't treat it like a failure. Keep cheering her on. Sometimes the difference between success and failure in kicking an addiction is the support of a consistent, encouraging friend. You may be the only person who stands with your addicted friend through thick and thin. You may be the only friend she has at the moments she most needs a friend.

THE JESUS MODEL

If you really want to make a difference in the life of an addict, try helping him turn his destructive behavior into something that will fill the eternal void in his life. Jesus said, "I am the bread of life. He who comes to me will never go hungry, and he who believes in me will never be thirsty" (John 6:35).

We all long for the emptiness in life to be filled. Some try to fill it with drugs while others turn to money or food. You, however, can offer ultimate satisfaction to the addicts you know. Just as Jesus offered the bread of life and the blood of forgiveness, he gives you the power to offer his body to anyone in need.

Don't forget—it wasn't that long ago Jesus came into your life and cleaned your spirit of sin and unfaithfulness. Don't lose sight of the fact that "all have sinned and fall short of the glory of God" (Romans 3:23). It's one thing to accept our own failures and expect God to forgive them, but when it comes to accepting other people's failures, we sometimes get a little selfish with forgiveness.

From time to time God opens doors for me to visit different Christian schools and churches. I've spoken from pulpits in the Baptist church, the Presbyterian church, the Methodist church, and several Bible churches, and for the most part they've all been wonderful experiences as I watched the body of Christ do what it is supposed to do.

But I was blown away by an Assembly church I visited about five years ago. As I sat in the front row, waiting for my turn at the podium, the senior pastor announced an addiction recovery Bible study. The group met on Sunday nights at 7:30 p.m. He said, "You don't want to miss how God is healing people who were slaves to addiction." I was intrigued. "Where is this program? What do they do? How can I get involved?" I wondered.

I later discovered that a friend of mine led the group. He spent an hour telling me success stories of people recovering from sex addiction, crack cocaine addiction—you name it. He told me about the accountability system they set up, how they spent countless meetings just praying and confessing their need for God. He testified of God's power to remove addictions from the hearts of men and women. It was awesome. I asked myself, "Why doesn't this happen at every church?"

WHAT CAN YOU DO?

My friends and I used to sit around and talk about people who couldn't slay the dragon of addiction. You know: the town drunks, the potheads, and the people who were never going to amount to anything in life. We laughed at and mocked them. We took pride in the fact that none of us would ever end up that way. And in the process I think we made God sad because we didn't realize the potential healing power of a friend.

What if you went to your youth leader and asked to start a group where people who were addicted to drugs or alcohol could find sanctuary and anonymity? Wouldn't it be great to have a group of kids committed to the healthy lifestyles of their friends? Teenagers reaching out to other teenagers in a support group setting can be a powerful ministry experience. But it takes courage, it takes a belief in recovery, and it takes a discerning spirit.

In the meantime, stand by your addicted friends. Find new and exciting ways to show them the love of Christ. Help the people around you see that addicts are simply trying to find love in all the wrong places.

I am convinced that the church, caring friends, and Christian teenagers can turn the tide of rejection that addicts face in our society. If Christians buy into God's healing power, no one will need "Just Say No" campaigns because addicts will see people of love wrapping the arms of God around their necks.

/// CHAPTER 6 ///

LOVING THE SICK

"'I NEEDED CLOTHES AND YOU CLOTHED ME, I WAS SICK AND YOU LOOKED AFTER ME, I WAS IN PRISON AND YOU CAME TO VISIT ME.'

"THEN THE RIGHTEOUS WILL ANSWER HIM, 'LORD, WHEN DID WE SEE YOU HUNGRY AND FEED YOU, OR THIRSTY AND GIVE YOU SOMETHING TO DRINK? WHEN DID WE SEE YOU A STRANGER AND INVITE YOU IN, OR NEEDING CLOTHES AND CLOTHE YOU? WHEN DID WE SEE YOU SICK OR IN PRISON AND GO TO VISIT YOU?'

"THE KING WILL REPLY, 'I TELL YOU THE TRUTH, WHATEVER YOU DID FOR ONE OF THE LEAST OF THESE BROTHERS OF MINE, YOU DID FOR ME.'" (MATTHEW 25:36-40)

The leadership team of Kanakuk, Colorado, meets every morning at 7:30 to pray, share funny stories, and take care of the business of the day. Running a summer

camp might seem like "kids' play" from the outside, but when you're responsible for the safety, entertainment, and spiritual welfare of 160 kids, things are quite hectic ALL THE TIME!

One particular morning our team was celebrating monumental breakthroughs with some of our most difficult-to-reach kids when the phone rang. I rarely interrupt a meeting to answer the phone, but for some reason, on that morning I picked up.

"Andy, there's been an accident. You might want to sit down."

My heart sank. Before another word was spoken, my mind raced through dozens of possible scenarios: My mom? My dad? My brother? One of my friends back home? A coworker?

The caller continued, "Last night Greg Bettis was flying the company plane back to camp..."

I almost threw up in the middle of the conference room because I was sure I knew what was coming next. I pictured the plane's wreckage, my friend's lifeless body, his funeral, his grieving family.

"The wing clipped one of the big oak trees on the landing approach, and the plane crashed. Fortunately, Greg survived. He's in the hospital, and it looks like there are several broken bones, but we really don't know the extent of the damage just yet. We're calling everybody and asking for prayer right now. Could you guys lift him up in prayer this morning?"

I breathed a sigh of relief that my premonition had been wrong. "Of course," I said. "We'll do it right now. Thanks for the call."

I rejoined the leadership team and told them the news. My wife, Jamie Jo, started crying. The others stared at me in disbelief. And then we prayed...and prayed...and prayed some more. We prayed for God to heal Greg. We thanked the Lord for saving Greg's life. We prayed for Greg's family. We prayed for strength for Greg to meet the challenges that rehab would present. We prayed for Greg's ministry. We covered the whole situation in prayer—not just one time, but multiple times. We didn't stop with an "Oh, God, if it's in your will." We prayed specifically that Greg would walk again.

Even as we prayed, I had a sneaking suspicion that this wasn't going to be an ordinary event. You see, Greg Bettis is a godly man. His compassion for people is second to no other person I've ever met. Greg is the president of a nonprofit ministry called Kids Across America, an organization that offers world-class athletic training for kids all over the country. There's only one stipulation: You can't participate unless you live in the inner city. The mission at Kids Across America is to change the course of America's inner cities, one kid at a time. Each summer the organization works in the lives of thousands of kids to give them encouragement and a sense of self-worth and to equip them with the personal skills they need to survive in the inner-city environment.

I've never met a guy as selfless as Greg Bettis. He has dedicated his life to inner-city ministry. Beyond that, though, he calls his friends on their birthdays. He calls me on my anniversary. He asks me how I'm doing and is genuinely interested in my answer. He's the quintessential friend. And at that moment he needed people to surround him with prayer. He needed God's love.

We prayed for Greg that day—not in a "God, I wish you would" way but in a "God, I know you're doing something here" way.

LINGERING DOUBTS

I'll admit, I was skeptical about the notion of a miraculous healing. For me our prayers were a formality, a request for God to watch over the proceedings. I balked at the idea that he would personally and supernaturally intervene in a health crisis. I mean, that's why he gave us doctors, right? And doctors are fallible. That explains why not everyone recovers from serious injuries or illnesses.

Could God heal Greg? I wasn't sure—even though I knew I should be. I knew I believed in the almighty God, the Creator who threw the stars into existence. But I wasn't sure whether he was still in the personal-healing business. And before I could pray with confidence for my friend Greg, I had to search the Scriptures to find direction.

My search took me to Luke 5:17-26, the story of Jesus' healing of a paralyzed man. The man's friends couldn't carry him into the house where Jesus was staying because the crowd was too great. So they cut a hole in the roof and lowered their friend to Jesus. Luke 5:20-26 picks up the story:

> When Jesus saw their faith, he said, "Friend, your sins are forgiven."
>
> The Pharisees and the teachers of the law began thinking to themselves, "Who is this fellow who speaks blasphemy? Who can forgive sins but God alone?"
>
> Jesus knew what they were thinking and asked, "Why are you thinking these things in your hearts? Which is easier: to say, 'Your sins are forgiven,' or to say, 'Get up and walk'? But that you may know that the Son of Man has authority on earth to forgive sins...." He said to the paralyzed man, "I tell you, get up, take your mat and go home." Immediately he stood up in front of them, took what he had been lying on and went home praising God. Everyone was amazed and gave praise to God. They were filled with awe and said, "We have seen remarkable things today."

I'd read the story before, but I'd always wondered, "Is it relevant to today's Christian life? Does Jesus still heal people like he did back then?"

My heart wanted to believe, but my mind couldn't accept it. I remembered theology classes in seminary

in which professors hammered home the concept of God's sovereignty. They told me he was the same yesterday, today, and forever. I thought about my pastor's sermon on Jesus' proclamation that he was the Alpha and the Omega, the beginning and the end. But I didn't know if I *really* bought into all that stuff...until I started praying for my friend Greg.

Day after day I lifted Greg up in prayer. And in time I began to see results—gradual but dramatic results.

The doctors' initial prognosis was grim. Due to the severity of Greg's injuries, they told him he would never walk again. But Greg wouldn't hear of it. So he endured surgery after surgery, medication after medication, rehab session after rehab session. His spirit never flagged. I never heard him complain once.

And through it all I (and countless others) kept praying.

I recently saw Greg at his daughter's wedding. As the organist played "Here Comes the Bride," I watched as Greg walked his daughter down the aisle to her eager groom. With a smile on his face, Greg gave his daughter away. He fulfilled his lifelong dream to be the father of the bride.

Don't be deceived: Greg still struggles. He's walking today, but with a limp. Although it's apparent God is working in his life both physically and spiritually, Greg wasn't instantaneously healed. Yet he is a living miracle. The Lord allowed him to survive a plane wreck.

  **LOVE THIS!**

And through Greg's life-changing encounter, the Lord allowed me to experience the power of prayer. I realize now that it's not my job to question God. It's my job to pray for people in the presence of the Lord. I can't heal anyone physically; but spiritually speaking, I can "lower" people to Jesus, believing he will heal them—just like the paralytic's friends believed in Luke 5. Some people may not have the strength or desire to approach Jesus on their own, so that's where I come in. I know if I bring them before the Lord, Jesus can take care of them.

James 5:14-15 says, "Is any one of you sick? He should call the elders of the church to pray over him and anoint him with oil in the name of the Lord. And the prayer offered in faith will make the sick person well; the Lord will raise him up. If he has sinned, he will be forgiven."

SETH'S STORY

If you think a man who survives a plane crash is a miracle, let me tell you about another friend.

Three years ago a young, aggressive teenager named Seth came to our camp. Seth came from a loving family who wanted him to spread his wings a bit and be exposed to Christian friends. Seth didn't have any major issues for us to deal with. He didn't have any horrible addictions. He was just a teenager living life to the fullest.

We spend a large portion of our time at camp teaching teenagers how to defend their faith. I start by teaching the Christian worldview and basic apologetics. Then we move on to more practical topics like dating, the media, and other issues teenagers deal with in the jungle of high school.

It's amazing to watch kids come to camp looking for a mountaintop high, both physically and spiritually, and leaving with a head full of God and a heart loaded with compassion.

I began my introduction to Christian worldviews that summer by briefly touching on atheism and the social responses an atheist has to give to live consistently with his or her belief.

Immediately following the session, Seth came to me and declared his devout belief in atheism. "I just don't believe in God," he declared.

"That's cool, pal," I replied. "You don't have to believe what I believe, and I'm not going to force you to believe anything you don't want to believe. I will, however, force you to think through your worldview and help you give explanations to hard questions you're going to face when you get to college. So don't close your mind just yet. Let's take this journey together and see if the Christian life makes any sense."

Reluctantly, Seth went back to his seat, bent on being an atheist. For two weeks he heard practical reasons why Christianity isn't a religion for idiots. He learned that faith has nothing to do with checking your

LOVE THIS!

brains at the door. He was challenged to think through things he'd never considered before. For the first time in his life Seth was exposed to Christians who wanted to search the heart of Jesus—and do it right.

After two weeks Seth's attitude changed. He showed an interest in learning more about the Christian faith. He decided there might be something after all to all that "Jesus stuff."

When the buses rolled into camp the next year, I saw a new Seth emerge. He told me he'd thought a lot about what he'd learned the previous year and had asked the Lord into his heart. He was a changed young man. Gone was the pessimism of the previous year. Seth's eyes were bright and full of hope. He started encouraging other kids in his cabin, and he became the highlight of my summer. I loved hanging with Seth.

Last summer Seth returned again to the camp to be a part of our oldest camper cabin. He'd spent the year learning more and more about the Bible and how it relates to everyday life. He was "on fire for the Lord." He was the first to volunteer to pray whenever he had the opportunity. He mentored some of the younger kids and told them how Jesus had changed his life. Seth quickly became the highlight of my summer once again.

Three days after Seth returned home, he called to tell me doctors had found something wrong with his blood work during a routine physical exam. He didn't know what was going on but asked me to pray. "They think it might be cancer," he said.

When I hung up the phone, I felt a spirit of oppression settle over me. I couldn't imagine why God would allow something like that to happen. Seth was a 16-year-old kid with his whole life ahead of him. My faith, which I had always thought was solid, was being put to the ultimate test.

For two or three days I walked around camp in a daze, wondering, "Why, God? Why would you allow something like this to happen to one of my good friends? You could use Seth to reach hundreds of teenagers just like him." I couldn't shake my doubts.

One night my wife noticed I was still struggling with Seth's health crisis. She looked over at me and asked, "You tell all the kids to pray, right? Have *you* prayed for Seth?"

What a NOVEL IDEA!

I'd spent so much time worrying about Seth that I totally forgot to ask the Lord to engage the situation and heal him. So I started to pray. *We* started to pray. I changed the entire schedule at camp and invited the campers to pray with me. They came into the gym an hour before each one of our club nights and prayed out loud for my friend Seth, even though some of them had never met him.

I offered the following words to those who joined me in lifting up Seth in prayer: "God chooses to heal sometimes, and sometimes he doesn't. I don't know why he chooses the times he does, but I do know he asks us to pray. So for the next 30 minutes, we'll spend time praying, however you want."

What followed was a life-changing event. Together we prayed and prayed. Days turned into weeks; weeks turned into months. Still we waited on the Lord to work a miracle.

On July 15 Seth called. He sounded sober and serious. I wondered whether God had responded to our prayers. Had he done anything to heal Seth?

"Andy," Seth said, "I know three years ago God brought me to the camp so I would know who he was. I accepted him in my life and forever will be changed. I know you specifically prayed for me when I was an atheist. I know you prayed for me to grow in the Lord for the last three years, and for that I'm grateful. I know you guys have been praying for me at camp, and today I know the hand of God heals in real life. I went to the doctors today, and after a long series of tests they couldn't find any trace of cancer in my body. They had scheduled me to do chemo a few weeks ago, but now I'm healed, and they say I don't need it."

I started crying. The Lord did it! We had asked, and the Lord had healed. He had intervened miraculously in the life of one teenager from Texas.

The Lord continues to love the sick. He's still in the business of healing those he chooses to heal.

That doesn't mean we can expect him to heal everyone we pray for. Still he wants us to ask. Jesus

says, "You did not choose me, but I chose you and appointed you to go and bear fruit—fruit that will last. Then the Father will give you whatever you ask in my name" (John 15:16).

Jesus didn't necessarily mean that if we ask him for a new car, he's going to give us a new car. The apostle John said, "This is the confidence we have in approaching God: that if we ask anything according to his will, he hears us. And if we know that he hears us—whatever we ask—we know that we have what we asked of him" (1 John 5:14-15).

I don't know why God chose to heal Greg and Seth, but I do know it is my responsibility to pray for the sick. It's your responsibility to pray for the sick, too. I believe if we ask for God's intervention, knowing it is by his power alone that people are healed, he sometimes chooses to show us his power.

If you know someone who is sick today, don't try to avoid her. Don't close your eyes to the situation and hope it will go away. Love the person enough to pray for her. Ask God to do his work in her life. And if and when God chooses to heal the person, make sure to give God all the glory.

/// CHAPTER 7 ///

LOVING THE ELDERLY

"**B**UT IF A WIDOW HAS CHILDREN OR GRANDCHILDREN, THESE SHOULD LEARN FIRST OF ALL TO PUT THEIR RELIGION INTO PRACTICE BY CARING FOR THEIR OWN FAMILY AND SO REPAYING THEIR PARENTS AND GRANDPARENTS, FOR THIS IS PLEASING TO **G**OD." (1 TIMOTHY 5:4)

Devon lives next door to a man he knows only as Mr. Johnston. Every morning when Devon leaves for school, he sees Mr. Johnston, wearing his robe and house slippers, slowly making his way down his driveway to retrieve the paper. Day after day, month after month, year after year, the scene has repeated itself. Mr. Johnston always carries a red coffee cup with steam rising from the top. He is always accompanied by a tiny poodle on a long leash. The dog always seems to be searching for a patch of grass on which to relieve itself.

And Devon always walks past without a word.

Mr. Johnston is an older guy—60, maybe 70 years old. And though he's lived next door for as long as Devon can remember, Devon knows little about him. In the winter Mr. Johnston shovels his driveway by himself. In the summer he plants roses in the front garden by the porch. And that's about the extent of Devon's knowledge of his neighbor. He's never seen a wife, kids, or any other sign of a family at the Johnston house.

Mr. Johnston never talks to Devon. He barely glances at him. But when he does look, it makes Devon uncomfortable. He usually turns around and walks away.

It's not that Devon isn't curious about Mr. Johnston; he is. It's just that he doesn't have courage to walk up to Mr. Johnston and start a conversation. What if Mr. Johnston hates kids? What if he turns out to be a grumpy old man—or even worse, senile?

Besides, Devon has heard dozens of comments from elderly people about how teenagers are too loud or too fast or too bold or too hard to understand. He's not sure he's the right person to try to bridge the generation gap—even though he has a pretty good inkling that God wants him to reach out to Mr. Johnston.

Day after day, month after month, year after year, Devon watches Mr. Johnston get his paper. He watches and wonders. He wonders if Mr. Johnston has any living friends or family. He wonders if getting the paper is the most exciting thing Mr. Johnston does all day. He

LOVE THIS!

wonders if that's the way all people act when they get to be Mr. Johnston's age.

Devon arrives home from school one day to find an ambulance and several cars parked on the street in front of his house. A crowd is gathered on Mr. Johnston's front lawn. Devon walks over just in time to see paramedics wheel a gurney out of the house and down to the ambulance. Mr. Johnston is lying on the gurney. His eyes are closed, and he has an oxygen mask on his face.

A young woman approaches Devon and asks, "Do you know him?" Devon shakes his head and replies, "I live next door, but I've never talked to him." His words seem cold and unfeeling to him.

"He's my dad," she says. She tells Devon about a fight she had with her father long ago. She says she hasn't spoken to him for years. She describes how a police officer had informed her that her father had suffered a massive stroke. She looks off in the distance and comments, "I've acted like a child. I should have been here." And a single tear runs down her cheek.

Mr. Johnston stays in the hospital for the next few days. The doctors say he had a brain hemorrhage that impaired his physical abilities. As a result he has problems with his speech, problems with his balance and coordination, and problems controlling his bodily functions. After much soul-searching, his daughter decides to put him in a retirement community near her home where healthcare professionals can give him the care he needs.

Devon can't help but feel he missed an opportunity to get to know his neighbor. He thinks about the days and nights Mr. Johnston spent alone, with no one to care for him and no one to talk to. He thinks about the opportunities he passed up to do helpful things for his neighbor. He wonders what might have happened if he'd gotten up the nerve to share his faith with Mr. Johnston.

What would you say to Devon? What would you have done in his situation?

BRIDGING THE GENERATION GAP

Sometimes loving your neighbor means reaching out to people of another generation—people much older than you. Sometimes it involves providing physical care or companionship for someone in the last chapter of life's adventure.

The question is, how? How can you show genuine, heartfelt love to someone you have nothing in common with? How can you initiate a meaningful relationship with someone old enough to be your grandparent? Here are some tips to keep in mind.

1. Have no fear.

One of the biggest obstacles to creating relationships with the grandmas and grandpas of the world is fear. If you're not used to being around senior citizens, you may have anxiety about the way they look, the way they move, the way they smell, the way they talk. You

may be afraid of saying the wrong thing or having to listen to stories about the "good old days."

One of my earliest memories of being a performer comes from fifth grade. Our Sunday school took a field trip to the local nursing home. I expected the folks there to be like my grandma—exciting, adventurous, and ready to play at a moment's notice. Instead I saw people who were almost completely helpless. They needed someone to feed them, someone to push their wheelchairs, and someone to help them into bed.

I remember being a little frightened, startled by a stage of life I'd never been exposed to before. Our group had gone to the nursing home to sing Christmas carols, and I wondered if the old folks in the audience were capable of appreciating the time we spent practicing.

I lost sight of one of the basic needs every person in the world has. In our innermost being we don't really long for "stuff." We don't *need* big houses. We don't *need* fast cars. We don't *need* shiny diamonds. What we need is people who are concerned about us, people who care for us, people who love us. The folks in that nursing home may have lost their eyesight or their hearing or even their health. But they hadn't lost their basic need for love.

One of the greatest gifts you can offer someone is a genuine interest in his or her life. Many elderly people are especially grateful for the opportunity to pass on their personal history. If you come equipped with a sense of curiosity, a respectful attitude, and a

listening ear, you have nothing to fear when it comes to interacting with senior citizens. Work through your apprehension to become someone who is interested in learning about people from previous generations, someone who will tend to their needs, someone who will listen to their stories and laugh at their jokes.

The need for love doesn't change once you reach 60 or 70 or 80. Just because elderly people have lived a long life and experienced an adventurous journey doesn't mean they lack the feelings and emotions you feel from day to day. They want to be loved just like you. Don't fear embarrassment. Don't fear rejection. Be confident and know that when you spend time with someone from an older generation, you are meeting one of his or her deepest needs.

2. Waste no time.

I met my wife in college when her grandfather was still alive. (Her grandmother is still alive at 88 and acting like a teenager.) Before I met him, I heard countless stories about "Pappy." How he had kayaked the seven most dangerous rivers in the United States...when he was 75 years old. How he had been a gunner during World War II. How he had taught hand-to-hand combat on Navy ships. How he had become a legend in Kanakuk circles.

I met Pappy for the first time when he was 79 years old. I'll never forget it. He shook my hand, looked me in the eyes as only Pappy could do, and made me feel truly welcome—even though I was just a punk college student dating his prized granddaughter.

Every time I visited his house on Whippoorwill Hill, he would pour me a cup of coffee and tell me the most outrageous stories I'd ever heard. I don't know if they were all true or not, but the man knew how to hold my attention. I remember sitting at the foot of his old blue leather chair, listening for hours as he told about all the history he'd lived. He told stories about the war, how he met Gram, the old days of the camping business, and how he loved to build stuff. Every story session always went back to some building he built back in the good old days.

With each visit I was happy to learn about the past, but I wanted to learn more about the man telling the story. I knew Pappy had graduated from USC with a degree in engineering. I also knew he loved to construct buildings. So I went down to the local hardware store and purchased a set of building plans for a garage-style barn to be built beside my house.

I took the plans straight to Pappy's house. I knocked on the door, and he welcomed me in with his usual warm smile. "Can I get you some coffee?" he asked. I walked in with the plans under my arm. When we reached the kitchen table, I rolled them out. "What are those for, Boy?" (He always called me "Boy"—not in a derogatory way but as a term of endearment.) I asked if he would teach me how to build the barn. His face immediately lit up, and he asked, "When do we start?"

For the next few months we worked on the barn, and I learned a lot about the man his friends called Spike. He was super funny. He was incredibly creative.

And he didn't mind taking time out of his life to teach me a few things about building. He showed me the power of patience, the value of precision, and the price for making something nice. He helped me understand how to create foundations, how to build walls, and how to measure for roofing structures. It was one of the greatest times in my life.

In the fall of the next year Pappy fell down a few stairs and broke his hip. The doctors performed a surgery they hoped would help him walk again; but for whatever reason, after the surgery Pappy was never the same again.

The vibrant man I knew who had climbed ladders to build my barn was suddenly confined to a wheelchair. His speech started to slur after a couple of months. Eventually he needed in-home, round-the-clock nursing care. I visited Pappy a few times, but every time I went, I was convinced he wasn't the same man I had known just a couple of months earlier.

As Pappy's days grew to a close, I spent less and less time at his house. I just couldn't bring myself to watch a man deteriorate and die. It was hard for me, so I stopped going. Only now do I realize how selfish I was and what a terrible mistake I made.

Pappy needed a friend, and I wasn't there for him. I was too wrapped up in my own feelings to look at his circumstances and truly love him like I should have. For that I'm sorry and ashamed. But I know Pappy's in heaven, and when I get there, the first thing I'm going

LOVE THIS!

to do when I see him is apologize for being so incredibly selfish.

I realize now that on this journey, this life isn't about me. It's not about how I feel. It's not about how much I work or how much I do. It's about the people I touch along the way.

Several students I talk with struggle with the idea of visiting nursing homes or hanging out with senior citizens. They believe it's a waste of time, that the people in the home probably won't remember their visits anyway.

I tell them what I'm telling you: Don't make the same mistake I did. People are people, whether they are nine or 90. Go to the nursing home. Watch the faces of the people there. See the kind of hope and comfort you bring them. Don't be like me. Don't sit on the sidelines when you have so little time to waste.

3. Offer a biblical response.

James 1:27 says, "Religion that God our Father accepts as pure and faultless is this: to look after orphans and widows in their distress and to keep oneself from being polluted by the world."

James refers to orphans and widows, but I wonder if he doesn't also mean to include all people who need someone else to help them to the end of life's journey. Orphans and widows need help because they lack someone to stand beside them through hard times.

They need someone to provide for them. They need someone to love them.

I think the elderly fall into the same category. They need love. And the good news is, it's easy to give. I enjoy calling Gram on the phone and asking her about what's going on in her world. I love taking over truckloads of cut timber so she can have a warm fire to read beside at night. I love taking my kids over to spend the day or night so Gram can have fun times with the family. I'm not the greatest provider, but I love doing what I can.

Jesus gave us the model to follow. During his earthly ministry he recognized the needs of people—both young and old—and worked to meet those needs. You can do the same thing for elderly people in your area. If you're unsure about their needs, try putting yourself in their position. Look at life from their perspective.

Consider the mixed emotions you might experience as you face your final years on this planet. Think about what it will be like to wonder whether you did everything God intended you to do with your life. Once you have an idea of how a person might feel, you can take steps to meet his or her needs.

4. Ignore social pressure.

In our culture, youth is everything. Look at the faces on popular magazines or the hottest celebrities in Hollywood. Chances are you won't find a senior citizen among them. That's because age is treated as an enemy—something to hide, something to fear, and something to run from.

Retailers offer creams to make wrinkles vanish, makeup to hide age spots, and workout programs designed to keep people young. Our culture places a priority on preserving youth for as long as possible, and I don't know why. In fact, I think we've got it all backward.

Perhaps it's because I'm starting to get older, but I think age is something to celebrate. Age brings wisdom. Age brings discernment. With age comes experience, and with experience comes the confidence to face the problems of the world.

We can learn much from people who have walked the road of life already. We can avoid certain pitfalls if we are humble enough to listen to the advice of older people. We've been trained to believe that life's value diminishes as we get older. But nothing is further from the truth.

WHAT ARE YOU WAITING FOR?

Imagine an army of young people with the courage and commitment to spend quality time with the elderly. Imagine the impact we could have on our culture by going to nursing homes, visiting hospitals, or spending time helping elderly neighbors.

Who knows? If enough high school students and college students band together, we might be able to

LOVING THE ELDERLY

change the stereotype of teenagers in the minds of those who are most critical. Are you ready for such a revolution? Are you ready to lock arms and love the elderly?

LOVE THIS!

/// **CHAPTER 8** ///

LOVING OTHER RACES

"So God created man in his own image, in the image of God he created him; male and female he created them." (Genesis 1:27)

My friend James is a youth director in a small town in the South. He works in a small church in a town with a long history of racial problems. James had a vision. He wanted to begin a reconciliation ministry to help white folks appreciate black folks and vice versa. James saw a town continuing to oppress people based on skin color, and he felt the Lord calling him to make a difference in the community.

Segregation was one problem he encountered. White people lived on one side of the town; African Americans lived on the other. White people shopped at one grocery store; blacks shopped at another. White people bought gas at one service station; blacks at another.

His first day at church James stared out at a congregation made up of white people. There were no people of color in attendance. He said it was the whitest service he'd ever been to. That's when James realized his task was going to be harder than he first thought. He was going to take a lot of people for a long ride toward racial reconciliation, but he knew that with God at the helm of his ministry, anything was possible (see Mark 10:27).

His first battleground in the quest for reconciliation was the church's youth group. He believed that if he could convince young people to begin accepting each other as equals rather than judging each other based on skin color, he could ignite a revolution. After all, he reasoned, how could a mom object if her white son's best friend happened to be African American? Little did James realize the depth at which racism impacts the human soul.

James' first strategy was to organize a weekly "pool extravaganza"—a time when kids in the neighborhood could swim at the local country club. The parents in the neighborhood liked James because he was trustworthy—and willing to entertain their kids for them. The church appreciated his ministry because of the rising attendance numbers at youth group.

James was well on his way to revolution. All he had to do was figure out a way to get the kids into the country club pool. The country club was the center of society. His plan was to start at the top of the social ladder and allow the revolution to trickle down to the "common folks."

LOVE THIS!

This particular club was of the "old school" variety, a place for business executives, housewives looking for something to do while the kids were in school, and a thriving golf community. In attitude and attire it was strictly formal.

While James was planning his pool extravaganza, he met a man at church who expressed an interest in helping the youth group. In conversation James learned that the man was the acting president of the country club. James knew for sure the Lord was at work.

Finally, one Sunday morning James was able to announce to the youth group, "Tomorrow is going to be our first pool extravaganza!" As an added incentive, James told the kids that if they all showed up, he would do his famous belly flop for them. He knew the belly flop would bring them out every time. The group cheered with excitement and chanted, "Belly flop! Belly flop! Belly flop!"

James posted a sign-up sheet at the back of the meeting room. By the end of the meeting the sheet was filled. White kids signed up. Black kids signed up. Middle Eastern kids signed up. As far as James was concerned, that sheet was confirmation that he was making headway in introducing racial harmony to his little southern town.

Monday morning rolled around, and James took the church minibus around the neighborhood to pick up all the kids on the list. He picked up Jenny, Sally, Susie, and John. He stopped by Mark's house and convinced Mark's mother it was okay for him to hang out with the white kids from the church. Jane's mom saw the mixture of kids on the bus and decided Jane had some reading to do to complete her summer reading list. James knew her decision was racially motivated, but it didn't deter him from his mission. He was doing God's work, and he was going to show that small town the importance of diversity.

By 11:30 the bus was full. The kids were excited to be heading to the exclusive country club for their first-ever pool extravaganza.

James pulled the church bus into the fancy circle driveway and got out to tell the valet what was going on. With obvious disgust the valet told James he might want to park the bus down the hill—*way* down the hill. But James wouldn't be deterred. He knew God had his hand on this situation.

James told the kids to get off the bus, and they cheered once again. A doorman dressed in a white tux-edo looked at the group suspiciously. But when James mentioned the name of the club member who attended the church, he snapped into action and opened the door. And for the first time in some of their lives the kids were privy to the fanciest place in town.

Great chandeliers lined the hallway. The walls were made of an exotic mahogany. Paintings of the members hung all around. The smell of gourmet food wafted through open doorways. The kids looked around as though they had just landed on a different planet, but not James. He kept on task. He was going to the pool, and nobody was going to stop him.

LOVE THIS!

As they rounded the last corner on their way to the pool, another man dressed in a white tuxedo stopped them. "I'm sorry, sir, the pool is in need of cleaning," he said. "You'll have to come back some other time."

James looked out the window and saw a white kid jump off the high dive. "But it looks like you guys are open," he pointed out.

"I'm sorry, sir," came the reply. "You'll have to come back another day."

"I don't understand," James said. "Mr. Jacobson gave us permission to come here. We're with the local church, and we just want to swim for a while." The tension in the air grew thick. James was on a mission, and he couldn't believe the man was going to be the final wall to keep the kids out of the pool.

"Sir, you don't understand," the man insisted. "You MUST come back some other time."

James silently looked at his group of kids—whites, blacks, and Middle Easterners—and immediately understood the problem. He asked the kids to gather outside the building, where they would discuss what was happening. With towels draped around their necks the kids hung their heads and slowly walked back to the bus.

When James joined them, he explained, "This is what happens when you look at someone who appears different from you. When you hold a grudge for no other reason than the color of someone's skin, jealousy and fear shape your behavior and dictate your decisions. It's not something to seek revenge over, but if you want to change this town, we MUST stick together." He said he gave his speech as if he were Abraham Lincoln trying to convince a nation to change its behavior.

James told me he might have expected such treatment in the 1950s, but not in 2004. He could not believe there were still organizations in the United States so racist that they would refuse to let people use their facilities based on skin color. To be honest, I couldn't believe it either.

FIGHTING RACISM

I suppose our reaction to people of different colors largely depends on our environment growing up. African Americans who are exposed to white people from an early age usually don't have a lot of problems relating to white people. Likewise, white people who are exposed to, say, Hispanics from an early age usually don't have issues with Hispanics.

So why, in such a culturally diverse nation, does racism still have a foothold? Why can't we get past skin color and see people for who they are? Experts cite several different possibilities: ignorance, fear, family influence. None of them is valid, of course. And fortunately all of them can be overcome.

The question is, how do we take our charge to love others to another level? How do we love those who don't look like us?

LOVE THIS!

Galatians 3:26-29 offers some guiding principles: "You are all sons of God through faith in Christ Jesus, for all of you who were baptized into Christ have clothed yourselves with Christ. There is neither Jew nor Greek, slave nor free, male nor female, for you are all one in Christ Jesus. If you belong to Christ, then you are Abraham's seed, and heirs according to the promise."

God doesn't see skin color; he sees souls. If we're committed to following him, we need to learn to have the same perspective.

My friend Rick is someone who recognizes the truth of Galatians 3:26-29. Rick is the pastor of an inner-city church. He comfortably and confidently walks into crack houses, prostitution areas, and gang neighborhoods. He talks with whites, blacks, browns, and yellows. He doesn't judge people based on the color of their skin. Do you want to know why?

Because Rick cares about people.

It doesn't matter that Rick is the whitest guy I've ever met, a stereotypical Midwesterner. His number one goal in life is to reach people for Jesus—no matter what color their skin is, no matter what sins they've committed, and no matter what their family situation is.

He bails guys out of jail, sits with prostitutes, and witnesses to crack whores. Recently, he told me about visiting a known crack house in the inner city. As he walked up the stairs, he noticed guys were dealing.

Rick walked right up to them and asked, "Hey, guys, what are you doing?"

"Hey, Pastor Rick!" the dealers called. They put their drugs away. Some guys sat with him for hours, talking about their families and what was going on in their lives. Rick won their respect because he would not allow skin color or reputation to deter him from his ministry. "All people are going to heaven or hell," he told me. "I don't think God looks at the outside."

Rick is making a difference in the world—and you can, too (though no one is suggesting that you pay a visit to your local crack house). Racism isn't going to end in your community until you and your fellow believers start caring about people the way Jesus did.

John 4:1-21 tells the story of a Samaritan woman who went to Jacob's well to fill a water bucket. While she was there, she encountered Jesus, who offered her much more than water.

Usually, Jewish travelers went out of their way, literally, to avoid Samaritan territory. But not Jesus. He decided to walk right through the middle of Samaria. He knew exactly what he was doing, of course. His mission was to begin dismantling the wall of racism that kept people apart. And he did it by striking up a conversation with one person.

Do you think a single conversation could have the same impact in the battle against racism in your school or community? Would you be willing to give it a shot? Find someone from a different race—someone the

LOVE THIS!

prevailing attitude at your school tells you to stay away from. Strike up a conversation. Show a genuine interest in the person. Find out what makes him or her tick. Start a friendship.

Starting one conversation may seem like a small, insignificant gesture in the battle against racism. But don't underestimate the Lord's ability to do something grand and significant with it.

/// CHAPTER 9 ///

LOVING PEOPLE FROM FOREIGN COUNTRIES

"CONSEQUENTLY, YOU ARE NO LONGER FOREIGNERS AND ALIENS, BUT FELLOW CITIZENS WITH GOD'S PEOPLE AND MEMBERS OF GOD'S HOUSEHOLD, BUILT ON THE FOUNDATION OF THE APOSTLES AND PROPHETS, WITH CHRIST JESUS HIMSELF AS THE CHIEF CORNERSTONE." (EPHESIANS 2:19-20)

The love that Jesus instructs his followers to demonstrate isn't restricted by neighborhood boundaries, city limits, state lines, or even national borders. Acts 1:8 confirms the scope of our mission: "But you will receive power when the Holy Spirit comes on you; and you will be my witnesses in Jerusalem, and in all Judea and Samaria, and to the ends of the earth."

It's one thing to show love to someone in your neighborhood or community—someone you can interact with face-to-face. But how can you effectively love someone on the other side of the world? I can answer that question for you because I married someone who figured it out early in life.

When Jamie Jo was in junior high school, she saw a picture of a little orphan girl in a faraway country. Something inside Jamie tugged at her heart. She couldn't imagine a little girl growing up without a mommy and a daddy, having to wonder who would take care of her and how she would get her next meal.

Jamie turned to the one person who she knew would help. "Daddy," she asked with her big brown eyes blinking ever so sweetly, "is there something we can do for this little girl?" As you might imagine, Jamie's dad's heart melted, and he sprang into action.

He placed a call to a local World Vision organization. World Vision is an international relief agency with ties to almost every country in the world. The organization offers much-needed assistance in providing care for poor children and supporting people looking for work. It also sponsors an international adoptive program to facilitate worldwide participation in feeding hungry kids. Jamie's dad thought the organization was a good fit for his daughter. But Jamie didn't want to help just one kid; she wanted to help them all. She wanted to make a difference in the lives of all needy children. Her heart was big and her vision limitless. Her father knew deep in his soul that Jamie was capable of achieving her goal.

The following weeks were filled with creative brainstorming sessions as Jamie and her dad tried to think of ways to help children halfway around the world. They considered lemonade stands, car washes, bake sales, and other ideas but dismissed them all. They needed

LOVE THIS!

a grand idea, something capable of having a global impact.

That idea came one night as Jamie was lying in bed. "I've got it!" she cried. She jumped up and ran to tell her father about the clothing line she envisioned. It would be called "White Sands," and its profits would be used to change lives around the globe.

At first the White Sands line consisted of T-shirts and sweatshirts sold at local markets. But with hard work and divine intervention, Jamie's idea turned into a national phenomenon. Jamie was profiled in national magazines. Everybody wanted to talk to the 14-year-old fashion guru from Branson, Missouri, who was trying to save the world's kids.

Thus began Jamie's adventure of a lifetime—one that would continue for years and years. Her youthful idea grew into a successful business—one that used its profits to subsidize food for kids in Cambodia.

I met Jamie during my freshman year of college. As the Lord's timing would have it, we met the first day of class and soon became best friends. She was fun to be around. She made me laugh. When we were together, I couldn't imagine being anywhere else. I started trusting her like I'd never trusted anyone before. She helped me work through girlfriend issues, studied with me for my New Testament finals, and brought me lunch when I couldn't get away from the theater.

In November of our freshman year we were driving to the movies when she looked over at me and asked,

"Hey, would you like to come to Cambodia with me for spring break?"

I just about wrecked the car. "Cambodia? Who goes to Cambodia for spring break?" I asked. Panama City Beach, Cancun, or Fort Lauderdale I could have understood. But Cambodia? I told her I had to think about such a radical proposition.

Eventually, the thought of hanging out with a good friend and visiting a country I'd never seen before was enough to sell me on the idea. Jamie and I started making plans for our Cambodia trip.

Our route took us from Dallas to Detroit, from Detroit to Bangkok, and finally from Bangkok to Phnom Penh, Cambodia. Thirty-six hours after our departure we arrived on the other side of the world. I've never been more excited to get off an airplane in my life.

From the airport we drove down a dusty road to a small hotel in the middle of the city. Everything about the place was different from the world I knew. The people looked different. The food smelled different. Even the roads were different. It was as if the Western world hadn't touched that little country on the other side of the planet.

We spent time with the villagers in the north who showed us the business World Vision supplemented. The women of the village made clay pots to catch rainwater for drinking. The pots they didn't use were sold to other villages for a profit. It was a great concept.

LOVE THIS!

In the village the women served a meal of hot white rice and some sort of meat. When they opened the wicker lid that covered the meat, I got a whiff of the meal I was being served. I promptly jumped up and ran outside to throw up. Let's just say it took some time to get used to Cambodian cuisine.

The highlight of the trip was our visit to the national pediatric hospital that had been built with the funds from White Sands, Jamie's clothing company. As we toured the facility, we had a chance to sit with mothers whose children were sick. To see the results of Jamie's efforts—to stare into the eyes of the people whose lives she touched—was a life-changing experience for me.

We've been back to Cambodia twice since then. Both times we were able to serve the women in the medical facility. It's amazing to see how the Lord changed so many lives simply by planting an idea in the mind of a young Midwestern girl.

GOING GLOBAL

Unfortunately, "out of sight, out of mind" is a real problem when it comes to Christian ministry overseas. Because we're not personally exposed to the conditions of suffering people in other parts of the world, their plights often seem abstract and incomprehensible to us. That's why it's important for us Christians to remind ourselves of certain truths and responsibilities.

1. To whom much is given, much is expected.

God bless America, the land of the free and the home of the brave. I can stick my chest out with pride because I live in the greatest country in all of history. But because I live in such a country, I am held to a different standard, because of the role the United States plays in the world today.

I've traveled to Europe, Southeast Asia, Latin America, and South America. And everywhere I've gone, I've met people who admire our nation. They admire the way we do business. They admire the way we educate our kids. They admire the way we care about our people and take care of them in hard times.

Luke 12:48 says, "From everyone who has been given much, much will be demanded." The fact that the United States has been blessed abundantly with wealth and power means that our nation must lead the way in caring for the world's needy. If people are hungry, we are supposed to give them something to eat (Matthew 25:35). We have a responsibility to look out for those who are less fortunate than we are—regardless of where they live.

2. God loves the world.

There's no trace of exclusion or favoritism in John 3:16, which assures us, "God so loved the WORLD." He didn't restrict himself to one population or people group. He demonstrated his love for the entire planet when he sent his Son to die on the cross. God chose to send

Jesus—knowing what would happen to him—to spiritually reconcile all the people of the world to him.

David Sutherland is an executive with Morgan Stanley. He lives in Hong Kong with his family and works out of an apartment in the city. Each summer Dave sends his two kids to our camp in Kanakuk, Colorado. That's where I met him a few summers ago and discovered his heart for ministry.

Dave told me he works in global finance to support his family. His passion, though, lies elsewhere. After visiting a poverty-stricken village in the Philippines, Dave realized he needed to do something. He partnered with a ministry dedicated to alleviating poverty and hunger in Philippine slums.

The organization feeds 50,000 people a day. They've set up medical clinics to address the physical needs of people in the country, and they've partnered with local churches to address people's spiritual needs. It's an amazing ministry.

The Philippines is just one country. You could take a journey to Africa where the national poverty rates would blow your mind. People living on 30 cents a day are not uncommon in some sub-Saharan nations. The world has great needs. The good news is you can be a part of the solution.

SOLVING THE WORLD'S PROBLEMS

If God loves the whole world, how can you identify with his mission? Here are a couple of tips.

1. Think "ONE."

Bono, Brad Pitt, and other celebrities have jumped on the bandwagon of the ONE campaign. No matter what you think about the people who support the initiative, though, you have to admit that the idea has possibilities. (And, no, I don't get any residuals for promoting ONE.)

The campaign's idea is simple: It only takes ONE. One dollar a month from one person, when multiplied by the number of an entire population, translates into millions of dollars to assist the world's poor. Just think: If the population of your church gave one dollar, you could probably make a sizable monthly pledge to World Vision or Compassion International. One dollar a month.

If everyone at your school (assuming you have at least 100 students in each grade) gave a dollar a week for the whole year, you could sponsor the drilling of a well for a community in Africa and provide drinking water in places where children are dying every second.

If everyone in your community donated one dollar a day...well, you do the math! If you have 500 homes in your community, with an average of four people in each home, that's $2,000 a day! If you could keep people giving $2,000 a day, you could accumulate $730,000 over the course of a year. I know some international ministries that need less than $700,000 to run a *10-year* program! Imagine the number of people you could help.

Have you ever heard Ray Boltz's song "Thank You"? The chorus goes, "Thank you for giving to the Lord, I am a life that was changed. Thank you for giving to the Lord, I am so glad you gave." The song tells the story of a man walking the streets of heaven and running into all of the people who were in heaven as a result of his faithfulness. The first person he encounters asked Jesus into his heart as an eight-year-old in the man's Sunday school class. The second person he encounters was led to Christ by a missionary the man supported. At the end of the song Jesus takes the man's arm and leads him to a place where he can see the thousands of people who are in heaven because of his decision to be faithful with the little things in life.

What awaits you in heaven? How many people will be eternally impacted by the way you live your life? You don't have to create an internationally renowned clothing line. You don't have to arrange for the adoption of thousands of children. You just have to be one working part of the body of Christ in this world.

2. Evaluate your needs.

One of my best friends is a youth pastor in Springfield, Missouri. Every year his church organizes a campaign to raise money for the specific needs of its missionaries—the resources and equipment they need to do

their jobs in the field. My buddy involves his youth group in the fund-raising by targeting a specific need to meet. For example, if a missionary needs a sound system, my buddy makes it the youth group's goal to raise the exact amount needed for the sound system.

One Wednesday night I was standing in the back of his youth group meeting area while he introduced the new mission drive to the group. My friend held up a pair of expensive tennis shoes and asked the kids how many of them owned shoes comparable to the ones he was holding. About 40 hands went up.

"How many of you have two pairs of tennis shoes?" he continued. About 300 hands went up. "How many of you have more than five pairs of tennis shoes?" About 100 hands stayed aloft.

"Do you realize these tennis shoes cost, on average, about $95?" my friend asked. "If everyone who has two pairs of tennis shoes decided to do without one pair, we could give our missionaries $28,500 today. Isn't that amazing? We've spent over $28,000 just on shoes when there are kids living in orphanages around the world who need to hear about the love of Jesus."

I took inventory in my own closet and found I had five pairs of shoes sitting under my drawers. If I had used the money I wasted on my five pairs of shoes to support a missions organization, I wonder how many people would have been able to hear the gospel as a result. I wonder if my desire for extra pairs of shoes pre-vented someone from eating. It's a sobering thought.

My youth pastor friend raised over $80,000 in the fund-raising campaign. The group ended up buying a car for one missionary, an amplifier for another, and a big-screen projector for yet another missionary so that he could show the "JESUS" film to indigenous people.

The fund-raising didn't take much work—just a little vision. It didn't take much time either—just a small commitment to look beyond one's immediate needs and desires.

I'm convinced that if everyone reading this book would do without one pair of shoes in his or her closet, we could feed whole communities for years. It takes real commitment to love people you've never seen before. It takes real compassion to reach out to people you may never meet—the kind of commitment and compassion Jesus showed.

/// CHAPTER 10 ///

LOVING YOUR ENEMIES

"Hey, Four Eyes! Catch this!" Before the small third-grader could reply, a soccer ball clocked him on the side of his face. "Are you going to cry, baby?" the bully sneered. "Go cry to your mommy!" A stinging pain shot through the boy's head. His ears started to ring. A crowd of "cool kids" started laughing. Tears welled up in his eyes. He suddenly hated his dad for taking a new job and moving him away from his friends at his old school. For some reason he was having trouble making friends at his new school. He hated the kids there already. Their abuse was too much to handle.

"Look at her! Can you believe she's wearing that awful dress to school?" The girls snickered as they

walked down the hall to second-period English. They wouldn't dare point their fingers in her face, but they might as well have. Their words echoed down the hallway, clearly intended to be heard by the seventh-grade girl standing at her locker. The girl didn't want to wear the dress to school that morning, but her mom was working all weekend and didn't have time to do laundry. The girl's hair was matted because she didn't have time to get ready that morning. No matter how she looked, though, the other girls at school mercilessly made fun of her. Sometimes the girl thought about ending it all. She figured it wouldn't matter much anyway. She doubted anyone would notice if she didn't show up for school the next day.

"Are you serious? Check out that zit on her forehead!" Lucy knew exactly what people would say when they saw her. She pictured everyone laughing when she walked into class. Her body was changing in weird ways. That morning she had awakened to find a volcano in the middle of her face. "So much for my trips to the dermatologist," she thought. She tried to cover the ugly red bump with a heavy coat of makeup but to no avail. She braced herself for another day of laughing, jeering, and snickering from the other girls. "Why are they so perfect?" she cried as she headed downstairs to catch the bus to school.

Have you experienced incidents like those? Have you ever been the target of ridicule, cruel laughter, or bullying? Have you ever felt like an outcast because you wear glasses or braces...or because you have acne...or because you like music instead of sports...or because your clothes aren't right? Have you ever wanted to disappear—or make other people disappear?

THE OUTCASTS' REVENGE

Every high school in the world is full of imperfect kids. Many of those kids try to divert attention away from their own imperfections by drawing people's attention to the imperfections of others. That hurt-or-be-hurt mentality makes victims of some kids and bullies of others. In extreme cases it can drive kids to react in horrific ways.

On Tuesday, April 20, 1999, Eric Harris and Dylan Klebold, two students at Columbine High near Denver, Colorado, walked into their school with one thought in mind: to exact revenge on the people who made their lives miserable. At about 11:14 that morning the young men carried two 20-pound propane bombs (with timers set for 11:17 a.m.) in duffel bags and placed them near tables in the cafeteria. No one thought much about it because most kids brought bags to lunch. The two then went back to their cars to wait for the explosions.

But nothing happened. (It's believed that if the bombs had exploded, almost all of the 488 students in the cafeteria would have been killed.) Realizing their original plan had failed, Harris and Klebold implemented their backup plan.

Klebold, wearing cargo pants and a black T-shirt with "Wrath" on the front, was armed with a 9-mm

semiautomatic handgun and a 12-gauge double-barrel sawed-off shotgun. Harris, wearing dark-colored pants and a white T-shirt that said "Natural Selection," was armed with a 9-mm carbine rifle and a 12-gauge pump sawed-off shotgun. Both wore black trench coats to hide the weapons they were carrying and their utility belts filled with ammunition. Klebold wore a black glove on his left hand; Harris wore a black glove on his right hand. They also carried knives, as well as a backpack and a duffel bag filled with bombs.

At 11:19 a.m. two pipe bombs that Klebold and Harris had set up in an open field several blocks away exploded. Those bombs were intended as a distraction for police officers.

At about the same time, Klebold and Harris started firing their weapons at students sitting outside the cafeteria. Almost immediately 17-year-old Rachel Scott was killed and Richard Castaldo was injured. But the gunmen didn't stop there. Harris took off his trench coat, and both boys kept firing. They didn't stop until 12 people were dead and 24 others were wounded. Then they turned their guns on themselves and ended their young lives.

One of my closest friends was a counselor to some of the kids who were traumatized by the incident. He was privy to some of the FBI photos taken at the school immediately after the massacre. "Andy, it looked worse then any Vietnam War movie I've ever seen," he later told me.

I never knew Eric Harris or Dylan Klebold. I have no idea what they were like at school. I don't know if they were bullies or targets of abuse before the incident. What I do know is that when the news of Columbine crossed the ticker of the news station that afternoon, pictures of evil flooded my mind. I know the battle here on earth "is not against flesh and blood, but against the rulers, against the authorities, against the powers of this dark world and against the spiritual forces of evil in the heavenly realms" (Ephesians 6:12). But as far as I was concerned, those two teenage mass murderers were the embodiment of pure evil.

Surely when Jesus said, "Love your enemies," he didn't mean people like Eric Harris and Dylan Klebold. Did he?

The families of Columbine will forever feel the sting of death. Every time they look at the pictures in their hallways of the boys and girls who would be in their mid-20s today, they will be reminded of what they lost. No doubt many of them still struggle with feelings of anger and rage toward the children's murderers. Should they be expected to love the young men who took their most valuable treasures away?

It's a tough question, because our natural response is to lash out at those who take things from us. But that's not what God wants from us. Remember, he said, "Do not seek revenge or bear a grudge against one of your people, but love your neighbor as yourself. I am the LORD" (Leviticus 19:18).

Recently I read an article by Tom Mauser, the father of one of the students killed on that dreadful April morning. He wrote—

Shortly after Columbine, my wife, Linda, and I went to a meeting for parents of murdered children. The room was filled with anger and emotional gridlock. Perhaps it was easier for me because my son's killers were dead, but it made me realize that I had to pull something positive out of this tragedy. If I let it defeat me, the killers would have won.

In the first few weeks after the shooting Linda and I dealt with our grief by taking walks in a park next to Columbine High, and it was there that Linda introduced the idea of adopting a Chinese baby. We did so, as a way of honoring Daniel. Creating a Web site about Daniel was also an important part of our journey. Our goal is to honor Daniel with acts of hope and not mar our memory of him with anger or hatred or despair.

I don't know if Tom and Linda Mauser are Christians. I don't know what they believe about forgiveness. In all honesty I don't know how they cope with the loss of their son. I would be angry. I would wonder how a good God could do that to my family. Forgiveness is a hard pill to swallow when you can justify holding a grudge. But Tom and Linda Mauser are living examples of people trying to move past grudges and anger and rage. And for that, Tom and Linda Mauser will forever be the heroes of a horrible tragedy.

LOVE THIS!

ENEMY MINE

How do you handle life when enemies line up against you? When bullies make fun of your clothes or the zits on your face? Do you ever wonder why you, as a child of the almighty God, have to face such opposition?

Some Christians mistakenly believe that when they give their lives to the Lord, all things suddenly become good. But nowhere in the Bible does God promise a life of ease when you accept Jesus as your personal Savior. In fact, Jesus said, "If the world hates you, keep in mind that it hated me first. If you belonged to the world, it would love you as its own. As it is, you do not belong to the world, but I have chosen you out of the world. That is why the world hates you" (John 15:18-19).

Jesus warned his disciples of people who would respond to their faith with anger and hatred. Should we expect things to be any different in our lives? Jesus' enemies hated him so much that they pounded nails in his hands and feet and hung him on a tree to die. What makes us think we should escape a similar fate?

Chances are, your enemies will never threaten your life. They may never even physically attack you. But make no mistake: You *will* have enemies. Enemies are a part of life. Therefore, we have a responsibility to decide how we are going to respond to them when they show up.

LOVE THEM?

People who enjoy making life miserable for others share a few things in common. Insecurity runs through their veins like the very blood nourishing their body. They long to make someone else suffer to make themselves feel better. In dealing with such people, it sometimes helps to understand that they are hurting inside.

I'm not making excuses for violent or hurtful behavior, but the fact is, Jesus commanded us to love our enemies. He tells his disciples in Matthew 5:46-48, "If you love those who love you, what reward will you get? Are not even the tax collectors doing that? And if you greet only your brothers, what are you doing more than others? Do not even pagans do that? Be perfect, therefore, as your heavenly Father is perfect."

It's easy to love those who do good to us, but to be perfect like our heavenly Father is perfect, we must take another step toward love. We must love those who do harm to us. We have to love the Eric Harrises and Dylan Klebolds of the world. Their actions are inexcusable, but our response, according to Scripture, should be to reach out and love them.

When Al Qaeda launched its attacks on September 11, 2001, our country was enraged. People openly expressed their hatred toward Osama Bin Laden and the violent extremists who planned and carried out the attacks. Some of my friends bought gun targets with Osama's face on them to use at the practice range.

I went to church the Sunday after 9/11, and the sanctuary was packed. People came from all over the area, wondering if the end of the world was at hand. That morning my pastor delivered one of the greatest sermons I've ever heard. One of his points was, "We must pray for Osama Bin Laden."

You can imagine the silent response of many in the congregation: "WHAT? Pray for a killer? NO WAY!"

The pastor quoted Matthew 5:43-45, and the Holy Spirit began to convict my heart. I realized that it's not my responsibility to hate. Jesus calls me to love even the vilest people on the planet. Who am I to pull the trigger and shoot Osama Bin Laden? It's God's job to judge him. The man will certainly face the consequences of his actions upon his death.

Don't misunderstand me: In no way do I condone or excuse the man's actions. The Bible makes it clear that laws must be upheld and that there is a system of accountability for violating those laws. But none of that changes the fact that I am required and encouraged to love people like Osama Bin Laden, no matter how the rest of the world feels about them. Don't mistake me for a doormat, either. I do not advocate sitting by and watching evil people carry out their evil plans. But I do advocate loving enemies as God commanded.

GIVE THEM SOMETHING?

Jesus takes the command to love our enemies to a whole new level in Matthew 5:39-42: "But I tell you,

Do not resist an evil person. If someone strikes you on the right cheek, turn to him the other also. And if someone wants to sue you and take your tunic, let him have your cloak as well. If someone forces you to go one mile, go with him two miles. Give to the one who asks you, and do not turn away from the one who wants to borrow from you."

Imagine having someone in your life who makes fun of you all the time and constantly tries to embarrass you in front of other people. (Maybe you don't have to imagine such a person.) Now imagine that the person desperately needs a ride home...or tutoring in math...or money to buy lunch. The only person who can help him is you, which gives you the opportunity to get some long-awaited payback.

What would you do? What would you *like* to do? What would Jesus have you do? That third question is easy to answer. Jesus says to give the person whatever he needs. Sacrifice your own needs, if necessary, but do right by the person. Resist the urge to repay evil for evil. You won't be sorry.

If you want to know the power of God in your life, identify your enemies and start treating them like friends. In time you may find yourself with fewer and fewer enemies if you eliminate reasons for people to treat you poorly. I'm not suggesting that every enemy you've ever had will line up to join your fan club if you treat them nicely. But I am suggesting that many people have difficulty making fun of someone who is constantly looking out for their needs.

LOVE THIS!

REJOICE IN THEM?

In Philippians 4:4-7 the apostle Paul writes, "Rejoice in the Lord always. I will say it again: Rejoice! Let your gentleness be evident to all. The Lord is near. Do not be anxious about anything, but in everything, by prayer and petition, with thanksgiving, present your requests to God. And the peace of God, which transcends all understanding, will guard your hearts and your minds in Christ Jesus."

The natural reaction to that passage is disbelief. Is Paul serious about rejoicing in the Lord ALWAYS? *Rejoice* when life gets hard and people get mean? *Rejoice* when enemies single you out for abuse? Is that even possible?

Actually, yes, it is possible. But it's not easy. The kind of rejoicing God is looking for doesn't come naturally; it's a conscious decision, a choice to react in an unnatural—but sincere—way.

To love your enemies, you must make a conscious decision to rejoice in their presence. What could be more unexpected—more astonishing—than that? Our society conditions people to expect retaliation from enemies. When they see instead a "peace that passes all understanding," many people are intrigued.

Imagine what would happen if Christians made a global commitment to reach out to enemies with rejoicing in our hearts. To the drug dealer, rejoice. To the casino owner, rejoice. To the guy selling pornography at the local gas station, rejoice. To the people who steal from you, rejoice. Can you imagine what a thief would say if you caught him in the act of stealing and, with a smile on your face, said, "Just take it"? I'm not talking about condoning sin. I'm talking about reaching out with a spirit of rejoicing to an enemy.

If you're serious about living a life of obedience to God, you must learn to show love to enemies—and that includes everyone from school bullies to Osama Bin Laden.

I tell you this not as an expert but as someone who struggles with the Lord's commands concerning enemies. When someone does something to harm me or my family, my first reaction is not to rejoice; it's to express my anger and desire for revenge. Chances are, you face the same struggle. But if we are going to change the world, we must learn how to LOVE THIS! too.

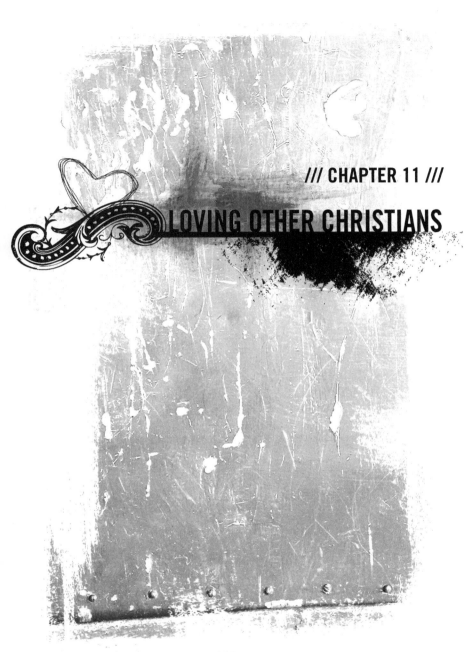

/// CHAPTER 11 ///

LOVING OTHER CHRISTIANS

"BY THIS ALL MEN WILL KNOW THAT YOU ARE MY DISCIPLES, IF YOU LOVE ONE ANOTHER." (JOHN 13:35)

Jack grew up in a small town in the middle of Texas. The town had a gas station on the corner of Main Street across from City Hall and one stoplight at the intersection of Main Street and Third Avenue. The most exciting thing Jack remembers happening in his town was when McDonald's announced it was opening a restaurant near the interstate, five miles away.

In the fall, high school football games were about the only weekend social option. The local feed store was the hangout for the over-40 crowd. Teenagers, when they weren't working on their parents' farms, raced cars and dreamed of moving to the big city.

Jack, however, was perfectly content with his life. His mother and father farmed 2,000 acres of fertile Texas prairie land, and Jack helped out as much as he could. Every Sunday Jack's family, like almost every other family in the small farming community, could be found at church. Jack looked forward to hanging out with his friends after church when they could play flag football in the field across the street.

The Sunday morning service itself was predictable, to say the least, starting with the same 70-80 people in the congregation. The pastor, who was from the old school, preferred to keep the order of service the same week after week. Every Sunday morning the congregation sang "How Great Thou Art" and then turned to greet one another. Ushers always collected the offering after the third song. And the pastor concluded every sermon with an invitation to accept Christ as Savior.

Jack learned a lot from the pastor. He knew most Bible stories by heart and grew to appreciate the hymns from the old hymnal. He learned about the authors of "Amazing Grace" and "It Is Well with My Soul."

When Jack was 18, he decided to go to The University of Texas. On his first campus visit he was amazed by all the local restaurants and student apartment buildings, not to mention the numerous outlets for fun on the weekends.

Jack moved into a small apartment just off campus. One of his first priorities was to find a church to attend. Like many college students, he began "shopping" for a church he could call home.

Some of his new college friends took him to a local African American church. Jack was surprised to see the choir swaying back and forth as they sang songs he'd never heard of. When the soloist took the stage, Jack forgot he was in a worship service. It seemed more like a hip-hop concert to him. He'd never heard that kind of music in a church before.

When the pastor approached the pulpit to begin his message, the organist remained at the keyboard. When the minister emphasized a specific point in his message, the organist would tickle the ivory keys and the congregation would scream out, "Amen! Preach it!" Jack found himself extremely uncomfortable with the outbursts during the preacher's message. He wondered, "Aren't people supposed to be quiet in church?"

The pastor kept preaching and the organist kept playing. Jack looked at his watch. 12:30 p.m. He'd never sat through a service that long before—if you could call that sitting. Every time the organist hit the keyboard, people would stand up and shout, "Hallelujah!" Jack was totally out of his element.

After the service was over, Jack and his friends went to the local Waffle House for a cheap afternoon college brunch. Jack's friends were excited about the biblical truths the pastor touched on during the service. But Jack had to confess, "I don't think that's my kind of church." His decision had nothing to do with race; it was just that the service was a little wilder than what he was used to.

The next Sunday another group of friends decided to attend the local megachurch. To Jack's eyes the building resembled a mall and the atrium looked like something out of a sports arena. He had been taught that churches were supposed to use their money to help missionaries around the world; but obviously, the megachurch had used considerable amounts on its structures (or "campus," as the church referred to it). The Sunday school class Jack attended offered incredible Bible-based teaching. The worship service was another study in diversity.

This time the songs were accompanied by an electric guitar, a bass guitar and drums. Jack had never heard the tunes, which were a long way from "How Great Thou Art." Worshipers sang of Jesus' miraculous workings in their lives, their sinful nature, and the freedom the Lord gave them. Jack found himself wanting to jump during the fast songs and close his eyes during the slow ones. He couldn't believe the number of people around him. It was more like a rock concert than a church.

The offering was taken in what looked like KFC buckets and not the golden plates he was used to back home. The pastor preached his message with passion and conviction. When the invitation was given, hundreds of people flocked to the front of the altar. The whole experience was overwhelming for a small-town, small-church boy who grew up listening to a lone piano and a monotone pastor on Sunday mornings.

At their weekly meeting at the Waffle House, Jack's friends asked him what he thought of the church. "It's just so big!" he confessed with a bit of sadness in his voice. "I like the message. I like the music. But how in the world do you get to know anyone in that church? I felt like a stranger."

The next week Jack decided to visit a church similar to the one he grew up with. He found a small country church outside of Austin that slightly resembled his church at home, so he decided to check it out.

Everything about the church and service reminded him of home. The pews were the same. The hymnals were the same. The order of service was the same. The smells from the musty dark wooden panels were the same. The pastor's preaching style was the same. After one visit Jack realized he had found a church to suit his needs.

What do you think of Jack's story? One of the churches he visited likely seems similar to the one you attend now. Whether it's at a small country church singing hymns and performing a service in a "traditional" way or at an African American church where the preacher is accompanied by an organ, Christians worship differently. No two ways are exactly alike, and none is necessarily any more godly than another.

SIMILARITIES AND DIFFERENCES

The pastor of my small-town church used to make jokes from the pulpit about other denominations ("The Methodists do this"; "Presbyterians believe that"; "Assembly of God people are a little crazy"). For the majority of my early life in the church I thought I was going to the only church that knew the right way to do things. We sang the right songs, our pastor preached the right messages, and our elder board knew exactly the right way to govern the church. As far as we were concerned, everyone else was doing something wrong and needed to see how we did things.

The only thing we were missing was new people in the church. What's more, in all my years there I never saw anyone come to know the Lord at the altar. We rarely hosted homeless people and never once offered an addiction recovery class. I can't remember one divorce support group. I do remember big fights over the color of the carpet—and whether or not young people would be allowed in the kitchen of the fellow-ship hall.

Isn't that sad? It's disheartening to think there are great people out there, worshiping God and commit-ting their lives to him, while their churches are caught up in arguments over carpet colors.

Isn't it time we stop bickering and start following Jesus?

Jesus told his disciples, "By this all men will know that you are my disciples, if you love one another" (John 13:35). Guess what? That Methodist church down the street is filled with people who are going to spend eternity with Jesus in heaven. As is the Assembly church, the Pentecostal church, the Baptist church, the Presbyterian church, and the Catholic church.

Sounds like the setup for a great joke: "A Baptist, a Methodist, and a Pentecostal are walking the streets of gold in heaven..." Can you imagine those people living near you—for eternity?

LOVE THIS!

If we want to show the world that Christianity is the one true faith, we need to start modeling the love of Jesus to the world. We have to stop the joking, jeering, laughing, and mocking and begin uniting as one body. Here are some ideas about how we can unite.

MANY PARTS, ONE BODY

In 1 Corinthians 12 Paul uses the analogy of the human body to describe how Christians should interact. He writes, "The body is a unit, though it is made up of many parts; and though all its parts are many, they form one body. So it is with Christ. For we were all baptized by one Spirit into one body—whether Jews or Greeks, slave or free—and we were all given the one Spirit to drink" (1 Corinthians 12:12-13).

We are all part of the body of Christ if we believe in Jesus the Son of God who came to take away the sins of the world. We are all baptized in the same spirit. Some people like to worship in different ways. Some have the gift of singing, while others have the gifts of playing music. Some people have the boldness to raise their hands in worship, while others silently kneel at their own pew in quietness to the Lord. It doesn't matter much how you worship as long as you are giving God the best worship you're capable of.

We need to stop pointing our fingers at different "body parts" and accusing them of being sacrilegious. Brothers and sisters united in Christ need to be mature enough to handle all kinds of worship. Dismissing people because of the way they worship is ungodly;

furthermore, it keeps the entire body of Christ from being able to witness effectively to the world.

Instead of falling prey to sarcasm and other unproductive ways of treating people, we Christians need to learn to celebrate the gifts of others. If someone's gift is singing, rejoice in her ability to sing rather than trying to put her down to make yourself feel better about the gifts God has given you. We need all parts of the body to perform their jobs in order for the whole body to function properly.

MANY VERSES, ONE BIBLE

For many Christians denominations act as fences—barriers that keep them apart from fellow believers. The desire to stay with one's "kind" is a powerful urge. And taken to its extreme, it can be a damaging urge.

As I see it, denominations are simply groups of people who tend to focus on specific verses in the Bible. Pentecostals tend to focus on passages that deal with the Holy Spirit's active work in the world today. Baptists tend to focus on passages that urge us to spread the gospel around the world. Methodists tend to focus on passages that call for community involvement. Presbyterians tend to focus on passages that affirm the traditions of the Christian faith. None of those groups is right or wrong; each simply has a different focus in its application of Scripture.

I'm pretty sure that when you die, God isn't going to quiz you at the pearly gates to make sure you got all the right answers to every issue. He isn't going to interrogate you on your views concerning predestination, soteriology, and epistemology. All of those issues are important to understand and work through; however, to think that God has a special place in heaven for the person who "figured it all out" and attended the "right" church is to deny the fact that God gave us unique points of view.

Look at Paul's words in 1 Corinthians 13:1-3: "If I speak in the tongues of men and of angels, but have not love, I am only a resounding gong or a clanging cymbal. If I have the gift of prophecy and can fathom all mysteries and all knowledge, and if I have a faith that can move mountains, but have not love, I am nothing. If I give all I possess to the poor and surrender my body to the flames, but have not love, I gain nothing."

It's quite all right to disagree with a fellow believer about the details of our faith. Just make sure that love supersedes your disagreement. You can still love someone you don't agree with. You can befriend people who don't cling to the same theological pillars you hold. Remember: We're all in this body of Christ together!

WORTH BATTLING OVER

I can think of a few truths in Scripture worth going to battle over: the fact that Jesus is the Son of God, the fact that salvation is available only through him, the fact that he came to serve, the fact that God made the world. Those are all essentials as far as I'm concerned. I will defend those truths until my last breath.

Other elements of Scripture are less essential to me. For example, I would not go into battle with someone who claimed the streets of heaven are paved with 24-karat instead of 18-karat gold. The argument would not be worth the potential damage it could cause to the body of Christ.

As you continue to work out your salvation (see Philippians 2:12), you need to determine which parts of your faith are worth battling for and which call for an agree-to-disagree stance. Focus on the elements that set Christianity apart from other world religions. Leave the rest for spirited coffee table discussions.

When I get to heaven, I plan to corner Jesus for a few millennia to ask him about things I don't understand. I want to know how he created the earth. I want to know why he refers to us as "predestined" children. I want to know why he healed some people and not others. I want to uncover the mysteries theologians have debated for centuries.

Until we have those answers from Christ himself, we must not allow debates and conflicting interpretations to divide his body here on earth. Remember that we have the potential—and the responsibility—to help the world understand Jesus' love through the way we treat each other. Let's not blow it over issues that have no eternal significance.

/// CHAPTER 12 ///

LOVING THOSE WHO MESS UP

"WHEN JESUS SAW THEIR FAITH, HE SAID, 'FRIEND, YOUR SINS ARE FORGIVEN.'" (LUKE 5:20)

Every summer Kanakuk employs 3,000 college students from all over the world. They come from almost every state in the union as well as from several different countries, all with one mission in mind: to help lead kids closer to Jesus. Our camp staff spends countless hours on the road, recruiting and interviewing, to make sure we get the right counselor in every cabin. We need ideal candidates to lead our outdoor trips, whether it's down a river in an eight-person raft or up a 14,000-foot mountain. Our "family," as we call our counselors, need to have the skill level to accomplish whatever activity they will lead, the personality to be a leader among teenagers, and a heart for the Lord.

It's hard to find just the right combination of personality traits. But after traveling to 250 college campuses around the United States, our organization has been known to collect over 3,000 applications for

about 1,200 open positions. It's a difficult process. Fortunately, we have the Lord working with us to help us find the right people.

Each would-be counselor has to fill out a three-page application and go through a rigorous 30-minute interview with one of our operations staff. They are asked questions such as, "When did you become a Christian?"; "What ministries are you involved with on your campus?"; "How is your quiet time with the Lord?"; "How is your relationship with your boyfriend or girlfriend?"; "What is your experience with kids?"

In the summer of 2004 we interviewed a young woman named Molly who had a deep longing to work at Kanakuk. At the time Molly was working with teenagers in a small town in Texas. She led a small group of high school girls. Every Tuesday night the group met over café lattes at Starbucks to talk about how to stand against high school peer pressure.

After Molly's interview, our staff did a background check on her that came back as clean as a whistle. So we hired her, much to her delight.

Molly was excited about spending the summer at Kanakuk. She made her plane reservations. She bought a new wardrobe for her Colorado experience. She told all her friends how eager she was to minister to teenage girls all summer. Working at Kanakuk was a dream come true for Molly. There was just one problem: Molly had a boyfriend.

The two had been dating for four or five years, and Molly was certain she had found The One. Molly and her boyfriend did everything together. They ate together. They played together. And unfortunately, they also shared a room together from time to time. Sex was the one area of her life she couldn't control.

When her boyfriend said, "If you love me, you'll do it," Molly believed him. So she compromised her purity for the sake of their relationship. She knew it was wrong, but she thought, "We're going to get married someday anyway, so what's the big deal?"

Needless to say, Molly didn't mention that during her Kanakuk interview. She was too embarrassed. She also didn't want it to hinder her chances of being hired, so she avoided the issue altogether. She didn't lie. She simply evaded certain questions.

About a week after having been intimate with her boyfriend, Molly started feeling...different. She knew something was wrong when she started throwing up every morning. "I knew it wasn't the flu," she told me later. "It just didn't feel like that."

A week later she started craving weird food combinations, such as pickles and ice cream or hot dogs and Cheese Doodles. One time she even went to a local café at midnight because she had to have some cornbread and refried beans.

Three weeks into her mysterious illness Molly decided to go to the doctor. The doctor immediately suspected Molly was pregnant, but she told him she

wasn't sexually active. She lied because she didn't want her family—her extremely conservative Midwestern family—to find out she had slept with her boyfriend.

After a battery of tests the doctor came back into the examining room and asked, "Are you sure you're not pregnant?"

Molly stopped breathing for what seemed like an eternity. The doctor could tell by the look on her face that something was up. "Look, why don't we do a pregnancy test, just to be sure?" he asked.

"Doctor?" Molly said.

"Yes?"

"Do we have that client-privilege thing between us?"

"Unless you're going to harm someone else or are a danger to yourself, what happens in this room stays here," the doctor assured her.

"Thanks." Though her problem was far from solved, Molly started breathing normally again.

She took the pregnancy test. The nurse said she would call in a few days with the results. That seemed like an eternity to Molly. She didn't know what to do. Tell her boyfriend? She knew she couldn't tell her parents. A mix of emotions ran through her. Desperation. Embarrassment. Shame.

LOVE THIS!

Not knowing what else to do, Molly took a walk. She cried. She worked out. She cried. She went to the movies. She cried. Finally, she couldn't stand the wait any longer. She had to know the test results.

As she entered the hospital, she tried her best to prepare for the news, whatever it was. If it turned out she was pregnant, she was determined to face the consequences with courage and honesty. If it turned out she wasn't pregnant, she promised to use a condom forever.

She walked into the nurse's station and asked to speak with the nurse who had administered the test. "Can you tell me the results yet?" she asked her.

"Molly, I told you I'd call," the nurse replied. "Now go home and don't worry. We'll deal with the results when they come in, okay?

"I can't wait," Molly said. "I mean...I have to know, you know?"

"I don't think this is a good idea," the nurse replied.

"Please!" Molly pleaded. "I have to know if I'm pregnant."

Molly stopped. It was the first time she had used the "P" word. Suddenly, the reality of her situation came crashing down on her.

Noticing Molly's obvious discomfort, the nurse ushered her to a chair and retrieved the test results. "Molly?" she said.

"Yes?"

"It's positive."

BAD NEWS

Jamie Jo and I had just moved to Colorado for our normal summer season. We were trying to get our kids adjusted to Colorado life with summer T-ball programs, vacation Bible school at a local church, and meeting up with old friends. Making the necessary adjustments after our annual relocation usually takes a couple of weeks, so we move out to Colorado before the other counselors arrive to get ourselves well-grounded in the community.

One evening after we had put the kids to bed, the phone rang. Jamie answered it.

"Uh-huh...oh, hi!" she said. I could hear only her side of the conversation, but it sounded intense, so I went out to work in my office and give her some privacy.

When I came back, she hung up the phone and looked at me. She'd been crying. I couldn't imagine what was going on. "Remember that girl, Molly?" she asked.

LOVE THIS!

"Yeah," I said. "Isn't she going to be one of our rock girls this summer?"

"Yeah...well...no...not exactly," Jamie Jo replied.

"What do you mean?"

"She's pregnant."

"WHAT?"

"Yeah, she's pregnant," Jamie Jo repeated. "And her boyfriend is supposed to work at K-7 this summer." (K-7 is another one of our campuses, located near Branson, Missouri.)

"What did you tell her?" I asked.

"It was the most amazing thing," Jamie Jo said. "For years I've been taught that sleeping with your boyfriend or your girlfriend is wrong. I've heard so many pastors and youth pastors give purity talks. It's almost like sex is the BIG ONE, you know? You can cuss, and nobody cares. It might sound a little rough, but the worst that happens is you get your mouth washed out with soap. You can drink, and nobody cares. You find a whole new group of loser friends, but it's not like people judge you if you drink. But being pregnant is different.

"Remember that book *The Scarlet Letter*?" she continued. "It's like that. You walk around with a big belly, evidence of what you did. If you don't have a wedding ring, people look at you funny, and they start judging you. It's like a man who sleeps with other girls doesn't have to live with any other issues except those internal ones he brings on himself. But a girl who gets pregnant has to live for nine months with a reminder. It receives nourishment when she eats. It kicks in her belly as it grows. You can't just forget about it."

"So what did you do?" I asked again.

"Well, first I told her she was right about not being able to come to camp. I said, 'There's no way we have the facility set up to care for you during a pregnancy. It's not safe, and you need to be at home.'"

"What'd she say?"

"Nothing," Jamie Jo replied. "I think she's still shocked that she's pregnant. The fact that she can't come to camp and fulfill a dream is setting in. It's going to be tough."

"Man, what a bummer," I said with all the compassion I could muster.

"But you know what?"

"What?"

"I told her to forget about her mistake," Jamie Jo said. "Forget about the disappointment. I said, 'You messed up. You know you messed up. Now it's time for you to forget about it.'"

"What are you talking about?" I said. "She can't just forget about it. In six months she's going to look like a whale. How can you just forget about it?"

"Well, everybody makes mistakes, right?" Jamie Jo asked. "And most mistakes we can cover up. Just because she can't cover this one—does that make her any more or less of a sinner than you and I? I told her to forget about it. She knows she made a mistake. She's repented of her mistake. She asked for forgiveness from her boyfriend and told him the relationship they were involved in was wrong. She asked for forgiveness from her parents. And most important, she asked for forgiveness from God. So I said, 'Forget about it. Mistakes are mistakes, and the biggest mistake would be to look down on this kid and be angry at him.' I told her, 'You only have your first baby one time in your life. Forget about the mistake and let's have fun with this pregnancy.'"

SOMETHING GOOD FROM SOMETHING BAD

I watched as my wife's big heart of compassion went out to the girl. She e-mailed Molly almost every day and started a mentoring relationship with her over the phone. Jamie Jo didn't even know the girl, but she knew what it meant to have kids. She knew what the pregnancy would bring. She knew what the delivery was going to be like. She helped Molly understand the wonderful life growing inside her.

Many people would have ostracized Molly. They would have condemned her for her bad judgment. They

would have blamed her for not being more careful, for not saving sex until marriage, for bringing disgrace on her mother and father. But not Jamie Jo.

Jamie Jo reached out to help her young friend understand what it means to be a mother. And in the process she offered an awesome example of the kind of love and compassion Jesus offers—and the kind he wants all Christians to offer.

What would happen if Christians learned to look past other people's sin like Jamie Jo did? How would unbelievers respond to us? How many hurting people could find healing? How many people would look at the Christian faith in a different light?

If you'd like to find out, here are some strategies for showing love to people who have messed up.

1. Remember that we are all sinners.

The Bible makes it clear that all of us are guilty of sin (see Romans 3:23). That includes everyone from Billy Graham to the pregnant girl in your high school. However, some sins (more specifically, the consequences of some sins) are more apparent than others. That doesn't make those sins worse than other sins; it just makes them more inescapably obvious.

If you walked around town with a television around your neck replaying all the sins you'd committed in your life—if people could peek into your innermost failures—you'd be humiliated. Unfortunately, some people, like Molly, face a similar scenario. The consequences of their sins are put on display for the whole world to see. The last thing people facing such public scrutiny need is another Christian jumping on the holy condemnation bandwagon, especially a Christian with sin baggage of his own.

Jesus says, "Do not judge, or you too will be judged. For in the same way you judge others, you will be judged, and with the measure you use, it will be measured to you. Why do you look at the speck of sawdust in your brother's eye and pay no attention to the plank in your own eye? How can you say to your brother, 'Let me take the speck out of your eye,' when all the time there is a plank in your own eye? You hypocrite, first take the plank out of your own eye, and then you will see clearly to remove the speck from your brother's eye" (Matthew 7:1-5).

Judgment is an essential component of knowing right from wrong, but when we ostracize those who need love and forgiveness, we are in direct violation of the life Jesus called us to live.

2. Reach out to those who need you.

All people on planet Earth have a desire to be loved. Everyone wants to be encouraged, thought of well, and even admired to one degree or another. People who live in sin are no different. In fact, their sin is often the vehicle they use to try to fill the emptiness and neediness inside them.

They don't understand that sex won't fulfill their innermost desire. They don't understand that drugs

won't satisfy their longing for meaning in this life. Often the sin in someone's life is a clear indication that he or she needs your Christlike love. Think of the guy who parties every weekend, trying to drown his problems in alcohol. Or the girl who gives herself to her boyfriend because the only time she feels loved is when they are in bed together. In their own way they are shouting, "Help me, please!"

Unfortunately, no one will ever walk up to you and ask, "Could you please tell me about Jesus? My life isn't turning out quite how I thought it would. I know God can fulfill my every need and desire. Could you share your faith with me?"

That's why you have to take the initiative to look for people who need God's love. Most likely, they're the ones being whispered about by other, less-than-helpful Christians. Once you make contact with people who are struggling with sin or moral failure, you must earn the right to share Jesus with them by becoming a dependable resource in their lives. Let them know, through your words and actions, that you care more about their future than their past.

3. Run from the temptation to judge someone else.

God alone has the ability to offer true forgiveness and mercy to those who need it. Therefore, God alone has the authority to pass judgment on people for the things they do wrong. That's good news for us because it frees us from the responsibility of having to determine whether a person is deserving of our love and attention. Since God is the judge, all we have to do is show love.

That's not to say we should take sin lightly. Look at Paul's words to the Romans: "What shall we say, then? Shall we go on sinning so that grace may increase? By no means! We died to sin; how can we live in it any longer? Or don't you know that all of us who were baptized into Christ Jesus were baptized into his death? We were therefore buried with him through baptism into death in order that, just as Christ was raised from the dead through the glory of the Father, we too may live a new life" (Romans 6:1-4).

Any sin is an extreme offense against God. And he's the One who will mete out consequences. We're the ones who can help people put their lives back together in the midst of those consequences. And if we take that responsibility seriously, we can make an immediate impact, as well as an eternal one.

When Jamie Jo reached out to Molly in the midst of her pregnancy, it changed my life—and I'm a Christian! Imagine the impact our actions could have if unbelievers saw us reaching out in love to people struggling with sin instead of condemning them.

If you allow genuine love to supersede your desire to pass judgment on others, you'll find that your friendships will become stronger and deeper. Your reputation will improve as well. People will stop treating you like a holier-than-thou scolder and start turning to you for help and advice.

People are tired of Pharisee-like condemnation; they want Christlike love.

/// CHAPTER 13 ///

NOW WHAT?

For a little more than 30 years, the Son of the Most High God lived among us on this planet. He could have come to earth as a king, a dignitary, or an important celebrity, but he didn't. He chose to become a lowly carpenter who worked in his (earthly) father's shop. He chose not to call attention to himself any more than was necessary. Instead he focused his life on doing the will of God the Father and loving other people.

Doing and loving. Those two words neatly sum up the nature of Jesus' earthly ministry. Jesus came to serve people—even to the point of death (see Matthew 20:28) He made his life a ransom for your sin and mine. He offered his body as a solution to the problem of sinful people having to spend eternity apart from God. He restored our fellowship with the heavenly Father.

Now *that's* a productive 30-some years!

A TALKER AND A DOER

Jesus talked a good game. Just look at any of his teachings in the four Gospels for proof. But he wasn't just a talker. He backed up his words with actions, as countless lepers, blind men, paralytics, deaf people, and victims of demon possession—not to mention a couple of dead people—in New Testament times could attest.

Jesus didn't form committees to identify and evaluate his ministry possibilities. He didn't consult board members regarding the specifics of his plan. Jesus came to earth to do the will of God—with emphasis on the word *DO*. Look at his words in John 14:10-11: "Don't you believe that I am in the Father, and that the Father is in me? The words I say to you are not just my own. Rather, it is the Father, living in me, who is doing his work. Believe me when I say that I am in the Father and the Father is in me; or at least believe on the evidence of the miracles themselves."

One such miracle is described in John 5:1-15. According to ancient tradition the pool of Bethesda had supernatural healing powers. It was thought that the angel of the Lord came to the pool occasionally to stir the waters. The first person into the pool, after the waters had been stirred, would be healed. As a result all manner of disabled and sick people surrounded the pool, waiting for their chance to be healed. One invalid spent every day for 38 years at the pool, waiting in vain to be cured of his affliction.

LOVE THIS!

Imagine his emotions one day when he heard a commotion near the pool. He could tell a crowd was approaching, one that seemed to be surrounding a single man. By the excitement in their voices, he could tell the man was something special. Before he knew it, the man was standing in front of him—the one people called Jesus. "Do you want to get well?" Jesus asked him.

"Sir," the invalid replied, "I have no one to help me into the pool when the water is stirred. While I am trying to get in, someone else goes down ahead of me."

Then Jesus said to him, "Get up! Pick up your mat and walk." At once the man was cured; he picked up his mat and walked.

You can bet that invalid was glad Jesus was a doer and not just a talker.

Matthew 8:2-3 tells the story of another encounter with Jesus: "A man with leprosy came and knelt before him and said, 'Lord, if you are willing, you can make me clean.' Jesus reached out his hand and touched the man. 'I am willing,' he said. 'Be clean!' Immediately he was cured of his leprosy."

The leper was well aware that Jesus was more than just a talker. He knew Jesus was a doer of marvelous, miraculous deeds.

You'll notice that Jesus didn't simply offer the man advice. He didn't say, "Well, if you eat right and exercise and take a dose of this medicine, there's a 70-percent

chance we can do something about your nagging leprosy problem." That's not the way God operates. And that's not the way he wants his followers to operate, either.

BE LIKE JESUS

In John 14:12-14 Jesus offers this amazing promise: "I tell you the truth, anyone who has faith in me will do what I have been doing. He will do even greater things than these, because I am going to the Father. And I will do whatever you ask in my name, so that the Son may bring glory to the Father. You may ask me for anything in my name, and I will do it."

Imagine doing some of the things Jesus did. Imagine being able to help people in a profound, life-changing way, as he did. You can—Jesus said so. For that to happen, though, you need to remember three things.

1. Your enemy wants you to be a talker, not a doer.

Ephesians 6:12 warns that our battle is "not against flesh and blood, but against the rulers, against the authorities, against the powers of this dark world and against the spiritual forces of evil in the heavenly realms." We have enemies in this world, spiritual forces willing to go to battle to prevent us from effectively ministering to other people.

That battle rages continuously. That's why it's so difficult for us to demonstrate the love God calls us to. The last thing our enemies want is for people to be

LOVE THIS!

exposed to God's life-changing love. Their fear is that if people see the kind of love God offers, they might start asking questions about how to incorporate that love into their own lives. Make no mistake—this is a battle for souls. The stakes are high, but you hold the keys to victory.

Your opposition wants nothing more than to fill your heart with fear. Fear of rejection. Fear of abandonment. Fear of being taken advantage of. Fear of the messy complications that come from getting involved in other people's lives.

DON'T BOW TO THAT FEAR. DON'T SURRENDER TO THE OPPOSITION. Remember, the Bible says, "Greater is he that is in you than he that is in the world" (1 John 4:4, ASV). Jesus said love your neighbor as yourself because he knows you can DO IT!

2. You must take the initiative.

Identify the people around you who need to be shown God's love. Your list might include a homeless guy you pass every morning on your way to school. Or a friend who's struggling with drinking or drugs. Or a girl at school who's been labeled a lesbian.

Once you have a working list of people to love, you can start brainstorming ways to impact their lives. You might have to sacrifice your time, your energy, your money, and in some cases, your reputation. (Immature Christians will always question your motives for hanging out with people who live in sin. They forget that Jesus did exactly that during his time on earth—and

faced similar accusations from the religious leaders of the day.) But the rewards of selfless love are always worth the sacrifices.

3. God wants you to be a doer, not a talker.

Several years ago Nike introduced a memorable slogan for its athletic brand: JUST DO IT. What could be simpler than those three words? Don't daydream about it. Don't talk about it.

Just do it.

The same slogan applies to the Christian life. James 1:22-25 puts it this way: "Do not merely listen to the word, and so deceive yourselves. Do what it says. Anyone who listens to the word but does not do what it says is like a man who looks at his face in a mirror and, after looking at himself, goes away and immediately forgets what he looks like. But the man who looks intently into the perfect law that gives freedom, and continues to do this, not forgetting what he has heard, but doing it—he will be blessed in what he does."

When it comes to showing God's love to others, there are thousands of ways to "just do it." If you know someone who needs encouragement, write her an uplifting note. Tell her what you admire about her. Let God's love pour out of your pen. Share the gospel of Christ through your actions.

A mentor once reminded me, "Between what is said and what is done, there is a lot more said than done." He was right. We can talk all day about people's needs without making the smallest difference in their lives. But one purposeful action, one physical intervention into a person's life, can be transforming.

Are you ready to transform lives?